Mediterranean Diet Cookbook for Beginners:

2000 Days of Quick & Easy
Mediterranean Recipes with 30-Minute Meals and a 30-Day Meal Plan
for Busy People

Jekson Goldman

Copyright © 2025 By Jekson Goldman. All rights reserved.

Legal Disclaimer & Image Notice

No part of this book may be reproduced, transmitted, or distributed in any form or by any means without written permission from the publisher, except in the case of brief quotations used in critical articles or reviews.

The content and information contained in this book have been compiled from reliable sources and are accurate to the best of the author's knowledge, belief, expertise, and available information. However, the author and publisher cannot be held liable for any omissions, errors, or damages arising from the use of the information provided.

Medical Disclaimer

The recipes, nutritional information, and dietary suggestions provided in this book are intended solely for informational and educational purposes. They should not be used as a substitute for professional medical advice, diagnosis, or treatment. Always consult a qualified healthcare professional or a licensed physician before making any changes to your diet, especially if you have existing medical conditions or dietary restrictions.

Image Disclaimer

All images included in this book are for illustrative purposes only. The final appearance of the dishes may differ from the photographs due to factors such as ingredient substitutions, cooking methods, presentation, and personal interpretation.

While every effort has been made to accurately represent the recipes and their outcomes, variations in appearance, texture, and color may occur. These differences are natural and should not be considered a failure of the recipe but rather a reflection of individual preparation styles and ingredient availability.

The author and publisher are not responsible for any discrepancies between the visual representation and the actual results.

TABLE OF CONTENTS

Introduction... 7
   Chapter 1: 30-DAY MEAL PLAN................ 9
Your 30-Day Mediterranean Meal Plan........... 11
BREAKFAST: CHAPTER 2: Protein-Packed Mediterranean Mornings...............................12
   ZA'ATAR-SPICED EGGS WITH SPINACH & SUMAC YOGURT.. 12
   CHICKPEA HASH WITH ROASTED GARLIC AND FETA... 12
   POACHED EGGS OVER WARM LENTILS & TOMATO CONFIT.. 13
   HERB OMELETTE WITH SUNDRIED TOMATOES & OLIVE TAPENADE.............. 13
   SMOKED SALMON WITH AVOCADO LABNEH AND DILL CRUNCH..................... 14
   TURKEY AND CHICKPEA BREAKFAST SKILLET WITH LEMON OIL...................... 14
   EGG WHITE FRITTATA WITH ROASTED ZUCCHINI AND PESTO............................ 15
   SAVORY COTTAGE CHEESE BOWL WITH GRILLED ASPARAGUS AND CAPERS...... 15
CHAPTER 3: Whole Grains with a Twist....... 16
   WARM FARRO WITH CHERRIES, ALMONDS & ORANGE BLOSSOM............. 16
   MILLET & OLIVE BREAKFAST CAKES WITH FETA CRUMBLE.............................. 16
   BARLEY BOWL WITH ROASTED APPLES & THYME YOGURT.. 17
   SAVORY QUINOA PORRIDGE WITH CARROT, TAHINI & CHIVES...................... 17
   COUSCOUS WITH ROASTED PEPPERS, OLIVES & SOFT EGG................................. 18
   SPICED FREEKEH WITH PISTACHIOS & LABNEH SWIRL...18
   BAKED BULGUR PATTIES WITH TOMATO-MINT CHUTNEY......................... 19
   CREAMY POLENTA WITH POACHED EGG, OREGANO AND SPINACH......................... 19
CHAPTER 4: Baked & Skillet Delights...........20
   SMASHED CHICKPEA & OLIVE TOAST WITH LEMON TAHINI DRIZZLE.................20
   SWEET POTATO AND EGG SKILLET WITH FETA AND DILL........................... 20
   TOMATO & GOAT CHEESE GALETTE WITH THYME SEED CRUST.................21
   ZUCCHINI PANCAKES WITH YOGURT-DILL SAUCE AND PINE NUTS.. 21
   BAKED EGGS IN EGGPLANT CUPS WITH PARSLEY PESTO........................... 22
   MUSHROOM & RED ONION TARTLETS WITH CRUMBLED FETA........................ 22
CHAPTER 5: Naturally Sweet Starts......... 23
   BAKED PEAR WITH RICOTTA, HONEY & TOASTED WALNUTS............................ 23
   FIG AND HAZELNUT BREAKFAST CLUSTERS WITH YOGURT CREAM.... 23
   WARM OATS WITH ORANGE ZEST, DATES AND PISTACHIOS..................... 24
   COUSCOUS BREAKFAST BOWL WITH APRICOTS & ROSE WATER................. 24
   ROASTED GRAPES WITH LABNEH AND ALMOND CRUNCH..................................25
   CREAMY MILLET WITH BERRIES, CHIA, AND MINT SYRUP...............................25
   FARRO WITH CINNAMON APPLES AND CARDAMOM YOGURT......................... 26
   OAT YOGURT PARFAIT WITH PLUMS AND POMEGRANATE MOLASSES.......26
LUNCH: CHAPTER 6: Hearty Bowls & Grain-Based Lunches.............................. 27
   WARM COUSCOUS BOWL WITH HARISSA CHICKPEAS, SPINACH & FETA...27
   FARRO SALAD WITH ROASTED EGGPLANT, TOMATOES & MINT YOGURT... 27
   LENTIL AND BROWN RICE BOWL WITH LEMON TAHINI DRIZZLE...................... 28
   QUINOA TABOULI WITH GRILLED CHICKEN, CUCUMBERS & POMEGRANATE................................... 28
   CHICKPEA & ROASTED CARROT BOWL

    WITH ZA'ATAR YOGURT...................... 29
    BARLEY PILAF WITH ROASTED PEPPERS, OLIVES & HALLOUMI......... 29
    BULGUR & GRILLED VEGETABLE BOWL WITH HERB PESTO................... 30
    MILLET SALAD WITH CHERRY TOMATOES, FETA & TOASTED PINE NUTS.. 30

CHAPTER 7: Light Mediterranean Mains. 31
    SEARED TUNA WITH WHITE BEANS, DILL & TOMATO RELISH....................... 31
    GRILLED CHICKEN WITH ARTICHOKES, CUCUMBER & OLIVE SALSA............... 31
    BAKED COD WITH HERBED COUSCOUS AND LEMON-TOMATO SAUCE.. 32
    TURKEY PATTIES WITH QUINOA TABBOULEH & YOGURT DIP............... 32
    SHRIMP SKEWERS WITH BULGUR, ZUCCHINI & PARSLEY VINAIGRETTE. 33
    SARDINE SALAD WITH FENNEL, ORANGE & TOASTED ALMONDS........ 33
    ROASTED SALMON WITH LENTILS, SPINACH & MUSTARD DRESSING...... 34
    GRILLED EGGPLANT STACK WITH RICOTTA, TOMATOES & BASIL OIL..... 34

CHAPTER 8: Nourishing One-Pan & Sheet-Pan Meals... 35
    ONE-PAN CHICKEN WITH ZUCCHINI, RED ONION & OLIVES........................... 35
    SHEET-PAN SHRIMP WITH SWEET POTATO, FETA & LEMON OIL...............35
    TURKEY & VEGETABLE RAGÙ WITH TOMATOES, GARLIC & OREGANO......36
    SKILLET LAMB WITH SPINACH, CHICKPEAS & CUMIN............................36
    BAKED HALIBUT WITH PEPPERS, POTATOES & ROSEMARY...................... 37
    EGGPLANT AND LENTIL BAKE WITH GARLIC YOGURT & PARSLEY............. 37
    MEDITERRANEAN MEATBALL TRAY WITH TOMATOES & CHICKPEAS..........38
    CHICKPEA SHAKSHUKA WITH SPINACH, HARISSA & POACHED EGG... 38

CHAPTER 9: Fresh Salads & Cold Lunches 39
    ORZO SALAD WITH TUNA, CHERRY TOMATOES & BASIL VINAIGRETTE.... 39
    ROASTED BEET SALAD WITH CHICKPEAS, DILL & LEMON YOGURT 39
    HALLOUMI & WATERMELON SALAD WITH CUCUMBER & MINT.................... 40
    WHITE BEAN SALAD WITH SARDINES, ARUGULA & CAPERS.......................... 40
    GRILLED CHICKEN SALAD WITH QUINOA, FIGS & WALNUTS................. 41
    COUSCOUS SALAD WITH ROASTED VEGETABLES & ZA'ATAR DRESSING..41
    LENTIL & TOMATO SALAD WITH FETA, OLIVES & FRESH THYME.....................42
    SUMMER BULGUR SALAD WITH SHRIMP, AVOCADO & CITRUS OIL......42

SNACK: CHAPTER 10: Baked Mediterranean Treats................................ 43
    BAKED FIGS WITH WALNUTS, HONEY & ORANGE ZEST................................43
    SPICED APPLE & DATE CRUMBLE WITH OLIVE OIL STREUSEL................ 43
    ALMOND & RICOTTA CAKE WITH LEMON SYRUP GLAZE........................44
    PISTACHIO & APRICOT BISCOTTI WITH ORANGE BLOSSOM.......................... 44
    BAKED PEARS WITH CINNAMON, GREEK YOGURT AND TOASTED SEEDS...45
    HONEY-SESAME PHYLLO ROLLS WITH CRUSHED ALMONDS........................ 45
    OLIVE OIL ORANGE LOAF WITH FIG CHUNKS AND ROSEMARY................... 46
    WARM PLUM CRISP WITH ALMOND CRUMBLE AND VANILLA LABNEH.......46

CHAPTER 11: Sweet Bowls to Share........ 47
    GREEK YOGURT MOUSSE WITH ROASTED GRAPES AND PISTACHIOS... 47
    CARDAMOM RICE PUDDING WITH ROSEWATER AND TOASTED NUTS....47
    QUINOA PORRIDGE WITH PEARS, POMEGRANATE AND MINT.................48
    CHIA PUDDING WITH ALMOND MILK, DATES AND CRUSHED WALNUTS...... 48

RICOTTA CREAM WITH SAUTÉED APPLES AND CINNAMON OIL..............49

COUSCOUS DESSERT BOWL WITH DRIED FRUITS AND ORANGE WATER 49

LABNEH WITH FRESH BERRIES, OLIVE OIL AND CRUSHED HAZELNUTS........ 50

WARM MILLET PUDDING WITH FIGS, HONEY AND LEMON PEEL................... 50

CHAPTER 12: Chilled & Frozen Family Sweets..................................... 51

FROZEN YOGURT BARK WITH STRAWBERRIES AND SUNFLOWER SEEDS..51

HONEY-LEMON LABNEH CHEESECAKE CUPS WITH SESAME CRUST.............. 51

ROSEWATER YOGURT POPSICLES WITH POMEGRANATE SEEDS.............52

ALMOND MILK ICE CREAM WITH CRUSHED APRICOTS & CARDAMOM. 52

FROZEN BANANA HALVES WITH DARK CHOCOLATE & NUTS........................... 53

SEMIFREDDO WITH TOASTED ALMONDS & ORANGE RIBBONS.........53

CHAPTER 13: Fruit-Forward Mediterranean Finishes.. 54

GRILLED PEACHES WITH BASIL AND BALSAMIC REDUCTION...................... 54

WATERMELON WEDGES WITH FETA, MINT AND HONEY DRIZZLE.................54

CITRUS SALAD WITH TOASTED PISTACHIOS AND YOGURT SWIRL..... 55

CARAMELIZED ORANGES WITH OLIVE OIL AND CINNAMON............................ 55

ROASTED APPLE RINGS WITH LABNEH AND ALMOND CRUST.......................... 56

BAKED GRAPEFRUIT HALVES WITH HONEY AND ROSEMARY SUGAR....... 56

FIG AND POMEGRANATE COMPOTE WITH RICOTTA CLOUDS...................... 57

PEAR AND PLUM SKILLET WITH CRUSHED WALNUTS AND OAT CRUST. 57

DINNER: CHAPTER 14: Family Classics with a Mediterranean Touch \\..58

LEMON-GARLIC ROAST CHICKEN WITH POTATOES AND GREEN BEANS......... 58

HERBED LAMB CHOPS WITH ROASTED CARROTS AND MINT YOGURT........... 58

TURKEY MEATBALLS IN TOMATO-OLIVE SAUCE WITH COUSCOUS..59

ONE-PAN CHICKEN THIGHS WITH SWEET POTATO AND RED ONION......59

BAKED FISH FILLETS WITH FENNEL, TOMATO AND DILL CRUST................. 60

STUFFED BELL PEPPERS WITH BROWN RICE, CHICKPEAS AND FETA... 60

BEEF & EGGPLANT CASSEROLE WITH GARLIC AND CINNAMON..................... 61

ROASTED CHICKEN LEGS WITH LEMON RICE AND SPINACH................61

GRILLED SALMON WITH QUINOA, CUCUMBER AND YOGURT HERB SAUCE... 62

BAKED PASTA WITH ZUCCHINI, TOMATOES AND PARMESAN CRUST. 62

CHAPTER 15: Sheet Pans, Skillets & Casseroles... 63

SHEET-PAN SHRIMP WITH CAULIFLOWER, BELL PEPPERS AND LEMON.. 63

SKILLET TURKEY AND LENTILS WITH CARROT AND THYME.......................... 63

ONE-DISH CHICKEN AND ORZO WITH CHERRY TOMATOES & SPINACH........ 64

FAMILY PAN RATATOUILLE WITH GOAT CHEESE & BASIL OIL..........................64

SHRIMP AND CHICKPEA BAKE WITH ZUCCHINI & RED ONION......................65

CASSEROLE OF WHITE BEANS, ROASTED PEPPERS & FETA CRUMBLE 65

SALMON TRAY BAKE WITH SWEET POTATO, DILL & LEMON......................66

SKILLET LAMB & COUSCOUS WITH CUMIN & RAISINS................................ 66

MEDITERRANEAN SHEPHERD'S PIE WITH GROUND BEEF & EGGPLANT... 67

SPINACH & FETA STUFFED SWEET POTATOES WITH GARLIC YOGURT....67

CHAPTER 16: Comfort Dinners Everyone Will Love 68

- CREAMY POLENTA WITH ROASTED MUSHROOMS & GARLIC OIL 68
- LENTIL STEW WITH CARROTS, TOMATO & OREGANO 68
- QUINOA & ROASTED CHICKEN BOWL WITH TAHINI DRESSING 69
- PASTA WITH SARDINES, CAPERS & TOASTED BREADCRUMBS 69
- BAKED COD WITH CHICKPEAS, TOMATO & SPINACH SAUCE 70
- FARRO RISOTTO WITH BUTTERNUT SQUASH & TOASTED PINE NUTS 70
- BROCCOLI & CAULIFLOWER GRATIN WITH HERBED YOGURT DRIZZLE 71
- BULGUR PILAF WITH GROUND TURKEY & ROASTED VEGETABLES ... 71
- GNOCCHI WITH TOMATO-BASIL SAUCE & CRUMBLED FETA 72
- WARM BARLEY & EGGPLANT BOWL WITH LEMON-PARSLEY OIL 72

CHAPTER 17: Gather & Share — Weekend Table Meals 73

- CHICKEN THIGHS WITH ARTICHOKES, LEMON & BABY POTATOES 73
- SPICED LAMB PATTIES WITH CUCUMBER SALAD & YOGURT SAUCE. 73
- ROASTED VEGETABLE PLATTER WITH CHICKPEA PURÉE & PITA 74
- ZUCCHINI BOATS STUFFED WITH TURKEY, RICE & HERBS 74
- SEAFOOD STEW WITH TOMATO, GARLIC & FRESH PARSLEY 75
- BAKED EGGPLANT ROLLS WITH RICOTTA & BASIL MARINARA 75
- GRILLED TUNA WITH FARRO, SPINACH & OLIVE TAPENADE 76
- FAMILY TRAY BAKE WITH SAUSAGE, ONIONS & WHITE BEANS 76
- GREEK-STYLE BAKED RICE WITH CHICKEN AND ROASTED PEPPERS ... 77
- CAULIFLOWER & CHICKPEA TAGINE WITH CINNAMON & APRICOT 77

CHAPTER 18: Grocery Planning for Mediterranean Success 78

- Grocery Shopping List for 7-Day Meal Plan 78
- Grocery Shopping List for 8-14 Day Meal Plan 79
- Grocery Shopping List for 15-21 Day Meal Plan 80
- Grocery Shopping List for 22-30 Day Meal Plan 81

Introduction

A Taste of the Mediterranean — A Journey to Health and Joy

Imagine sitting on a sunny terrace overlooking the sparkling sea, with the scent of fresh herbs in the air and a table full of vibrant, delicious food. This isn't a dream—it's the heart of the Mediterranean lifestyle. And you don't have to travel to Greece or Italy to experience it.

The Mediterranean Diet is more than just a way of eating—it's a celebration of fresh, wholesome food and the simple joy of sharing meals with the people you love. This cookbook is your guide to bringing the flavors, health benefits, and timeless traditions of the Mediterranean into your own kitchen—no matter how busy your schedule may be.

With 2000 days of quick, easy recipes and a complete 30-day meal plan, you'll discover how effortless and enjoyable healthy eating can be. Let's leave behind the stress of restrictive diets and rediscover food that fuels the body, lifts the spirit, and delights the senses.

What Is the Mediterranean Diet? A Way of Life, Not a Restriction

The Mediterranean Diet is consistently ranked as one of the healthiest diets in the world—and for good reason. Inspired by the eating habits of countries like Greece, Italy, and Spain, it focuses on:

Fresh vegetables and fruits

Whole grains and legumes

Healthy fats, especially extra virgin olive oil

Lean proteins like fish, seafood, and poultry

Dairy in moderation

Natural herbs and spices for rich, bold flavors

This way of eating is known to:

Support heart health

Aid in weight management

Balance blood sugar levels

Reduce inflammation

Boost energy and mental clarity

But it's not just about what you eat—it's how you eat. Meals are meant to be enjoyed, savored, and shared. It's food for the body, mind, and soul.

The Mediterranean Pantry — Your Key Ingredients

To get started, you'll want to stock your kitchen with simple, wholesome ingredients. Here's what you'll find in every Mediterranean kitchen:

Vegetables: tomatoes, zucchini, eggplant, bell peppers, spinach

Fruits: oranges, berries, figs, grapes, apples

Whole Grains: quinoa, bulgur, farro, brown rice, whole-grain pasta

Legumes: lentils, chickpeas, white beans

Seafood & Lean Protein: salmon, sardines, shrimp, chicken, turkey

Healthy Fats: extra virgin olive oil, olives, avocados, nuts, seeds

Dairy: Greek yogurt, feta, ricotta

Herbs & Spices: oregano, basil, rosemary, thyme, mint, garlic, lemon

This is a diet full of color, variety, and flavor. You'll never get bored because the possibilities are endless.

Quick & Easy Mediterranean Cooking — Simple, Delicious, Nourishing

Life is busy. That's why every recipe in this book is designed to be made in 30 minutes or less, without complicated techniques or hard-to-find ingredients.

From light breakfasts to hearty dinners, you'll find recipes such as:

Greek Yogurt & Berry Parfaits

Lemon Herb Grilled Chicken

Mediterranean Chickpea Salad

Baked Salmon with Garlic and Dill

Olive Oil & Lemon Zucchini Pasta

Each dish is crafted to nourish your body and satisfy your taste buds, all while fitting into your busy lifestyle.

Your 30-Day Mediterranean Meal Plan — A Simple Path to Lasting Change

To help you get started and stay on track, we've included a complete 30-day meal plan featuring balanced, varied menus that showcase the best of Mediterranean cooking. This plan takes the guesswork out of healthy eating and shows you how easy—and delicious—it can be to embrace this lifestyle.

You'll discover that in just one month, you can:

Feel more energized

Improve digestion

Shed unwanted pounds naturally

Stabilize blood sugar

Enjoy cooking and eating more than ever before

Chapter 1: 30-DAY MEAL PLAN

Day	Breakfast	Lunch	Snack	Dinner
Day 1	ZA'ATAR-SPICED EGGS WITH SPINACH & SUMAC YOGURT — p.12	WARM COUSCOUS BOWL WITH HARISSA CHICKPEAS, SPINACH & FETA — p.27	BAKED FIGS WITH WALNUTS, HONEY & ORANGE ZEST — p.43	LEMON-GARLIC ROAST CHICKEN WITH POTATOES AND GREEN BEANS — p.58
Day 2	BARLEY BOWL WITH ROASTED APPLES & THYME YOGURT — p.17	FARRO SALAD WITH ROASTED EGGPLANT, TOMATOES & MINT YOGURT — p.27	PISTACHIO & APRICOT BISCOTTI WITH ORANGE BLOSSOM — p.44	TURKEY MEATBALLS IN TOMATO-OLIVE SAUCE WITH COUSCOUS — p.59
Day 3	SWEET POTATO AND EGG SKILLET WITH FETA AND DILL — p.20	GRILLED CHICKEN WITH ARTICHOKES, CUCUMBER & OLIVE SALSA — p.31	BAKED PEARS WITH CINNAMON, GREEK YOGURT AND TOASTED SEEDS — p.45	BAKED FISH FILLETS WITH FENNEL, TOMATO AND DILL CRUST — p.60
Day 4	BAKED PEAR WITH RICOTTA, HONEY & TOASTED WALNUTS — p.23	BULGUR & GRILLED VEGETABLE BOWL WITH HERB PESTO — p.30	QUINOA PORRIDGE WITH PEARS, POMEGRANATE AND MINT — p.48	BEEF & EGGPLANT CASSEROLE WITH GARLIC AND CINNAMON — p.61
Day 5	WARM OATS WITH ORANGE ZEST, DATES AND PISTACHIOS — p.24	TURKEY & VEGETABLE RAGÙ WITH TOMATOES, GARLIC & OREGANO — p.36	LABNEH WITH FRESH BERRIES, OLIVE OIL AND CRUSHED HAZELNUTS — p.50	GRILLED SALMON WITH QUINOA, CUCUMBER AND YOGURT HERB SAUCE — p.62
Day 6	OAT YOGURT PARFAIT WITH PLUMS AND POMEGRANATE MOLASSES — p.26	ROASTED SALMON WITH LENTILS, SPINACH & MUSTARD DRESSING — p.34	HONEY-LEMON LABNEH CHEESECAKE CUPS WITH SESAME CRUST — p.51	SKILLET TURKEY AND LENTILS WITH CARROT AND THYME — p.63
Day 7	CHICKPEA HASH WITH ROASTED GARLIC AND FETA — p.12	ORZO SALAD WITH TUNA, CHERRY TOMATOES & BASIL VINAIGRETTE — p.39	ROSEWATER YOGURT POPSICLES WITH POMEGRANATE SEEDS — p.52	ONE-DISH CHICKEN AND ORZO WITH CHERRY TOMATOES & SPINACH — p.64
Day 8	SAVORY QUINOA PORRIDGE WITH CARROT, TAHINI & CHIVES — p.17	HALLOUMI & WATERMELON SALAD WITH CUCUMBER & MINT — p.40	GRILLED PEACHES WITH BASIL AND BALSAMIC REDUCTION — p.54	SHRIMP AND CHICKPEA BAKE WITH ZUCCHINI & RED ONION — p.65
Day 9	SMOKED SALMON WITH AVOCADO LABNEH AND DILL CRUNCH — p.14	SKILLET LAMB WITH SPINACH, CHICKPEAS & CUMIN — p.36	CITRUS SALAD WITH TOASTED PISTACHIOS AND YOGURT SWIRL — p.55	SPINACH & FETA STUFFED SWEET POTATOES WITH GARLIC YOGURT — p.67
Day 10	BAKED BULGUR PATTIES WITH TOMATO-MINT CHUTNEY — p.19	EGGPLANT AND LENTIL BAKE WITH GARLIC YOGURT & PARSLEY — p.37	CARAMELIZED ORANGES WITH OLIVE OIL AND CINNAMON — p.55	LENTIL STEW WITH CARROTS, TOMATO & OREGANO — p.68
Day 11	ZUCCHINI PANCAKES WITH YOGURT-DILL SAUCE AND PINE NUTS — p.21	CHICKPEA SHAKSHUKA WITH SPINACH, HARISSA & POACHED EGG — p.38	FIG AND POMEGRANATE COMPOTE WITH RICOTTA CLOUDS — p.57	FARRO RISOTTO WITH BUTTERNUT SQUASH & TOASTED PINE NUTS — p.70
Day 12	FIG AND HAZELNUT BREAKFAST CLUSTERS WITH YOGURT CREAM — p.23	WHITE BEAN SALAD WITH SARDINES, ARUGULA & CAPERS — p.40	SEMIFREDDO WITH TOASTED ALMONDS & ORANGE RIBBONS — p.53	GNOCCHI WITH TOMATO-BASIL SAUCE & CRUMBLED FETA — p.72
Day 13	COUSCOUS WITH ROASTED PEPPERS, OLIVES & SOFT EGG — p.18	SUMMER BULGUR SALAD WITH SHRIMP, AVOCADO & CITRUS OIL — p.42	ALMOND & RICOTTA CAKE WITH LEMON SYRUP GLAZE — p.44	ZUCCHINI BOATS STUFFED WITH TURKEY, RICE & HERBS — p.74
Day 14	CREAMY MILLET WITH BERRIES, CHIA, AND MINT SYRUP — p.25	COUSCOUS SALAD WITH ROASTED VEGETABLES & ZA'ATAR DRESSING — p.41	CHIA PUDDING WITH ALMOND MILK, DATES AND CRUSHED WALNUTS — p.48	SEAFOOD STEW WITH TOMATO, GARLIC & FRESH PARSLEY — p.75
Day 15	SPICED FREEKEH WITH PISTACHIOS & LABNEH SWIRL — p.18	LENTIL & TOMATO SALAD WITH FETA, OLIVES & FRESH THYME — p.42	RICOTTA CREAM WITH SAUTÉED APPLES AND CINNAMON OIL — p.49	GREEK-STYLE BAKED RICE WITH CHICKEN AND ROASTED PEPPERS — p.77

Day	Breakfast	Lunch	Snack	Dinner
Day 16	HERB OMELETTE WITH SUNDRIED TOMATOES & OLIVE TAPENADE — p.13	LENTIL AND BROWN RICE BOWL WITH LEMON TAHINI DRIZZLE — p.28	CARDAMOM RICE PUDDING WITH ROSEWATER AND TOASTED NUTS — p.47	HERBED LAMB CHOPS WITH ROASTED CARROTS AND MINT YOGURT — p.58
Day 17	MILLET & OLIVE BREAKFAST CAKES WITH FETA CRUMBLE — p.16	QUINOA TABOULI WITH GRILLED CHICKEN, CUCUMBERS & POMEGRANATE — p.28	CHIA PUDDING WITH ALMOND MILK, DATES AND CRUSHED WALNUTS — p.48	ONE-PAN CHICKEN THIGHS WITH SWEET POTATO AND RED ONION — p.59
Day 18	POACHED EGGS OVER WARM LENTILS & TOMATO CONFIT — p.13	SEARED TUNA WITH WHITE BEANS, DILL & TOMATO RELISH — p.31	RICOTTA CREAM WITH SAUTÉED APPLES AND CINNAMON OIL — p.49	STUFFED BELL PEPPERS WITH BROWN RICE, CHICKPEAS AND FETA — p.60
Day 19	TOMATO & GOAT CHEESE GALETTE WITH THYME SEED CRUST — p.21	BAKED COD WITH HERBED COUSCOUS AND LEMON-TOMATO SAUCE — p.32	COUSCOUS DESSERT BOWL WITH DRIED FRUITS AND ORANGE WATER — p.49	ROASTED CHICKEN LEGS WITH LEMON RICE AND SPINACH — p.61
Day 20	SAVORY COTTAGE CHEESE BOWL WITH GRILLED ASPARAGUS AND CAPERS — p.15	SARDINE SALAD WITH FENNEL, ORANGE & TOASTED ALMONDS — p.33	LABNEH WITH FRESH BERRIES, OLIVE OIL AND CRUSHED HAZELNUTS — p.50	BAKED PASTA WITH ZUCCHINI, TOMATOES AND PARMESAN CRUST — p.62
Day 21	BAKED EGGS IN EGGPLANT CUPS WITH PARSLEY PESTO — p.22	GRILLED EGGPLANT STACK WITH RICOTTA, TOMATOES & BASIL OIL — p.34	WARM MILLET PUDDING WITH FIGS, HONEY AND LEMON PEEL — p.50	SHRIMP AND CHICKPEA BAKE WITH ZUCCHINI & RED ONION — p.65
Day 22	MUSHROOM & RED ONION TARTLETS WITH CRUMBLED FETA — p.22	ONE-PAN CHICKEN WITH ZUCCHINI, RED ONION & OLIVES — p.35	FROZEN YOGURT BARK WITH STRAWBERRIES AND SUNFLOWER SEEDS — p.51	CASSEROLE OF WHITE BEANS, ROASTED PEPPERS & FETA CRUMBLE — p.65
Day 23	COUSCOUS BREAKFAST BOWL WITH APRICOTS & ROSE WATER — p.24	SHEET-PAN SHRIMP WITH SWEET POTATO, FETA & LEMON OIL — p.35	HONEY-LEMON LABNEH CHEESECAKE CUPS WITH SESAME CRUST — p.51	SALMON TRAY BAKE WITH SWEET POTATO, DILL & LEMON — p.66
Day 24	WARM FARRO WITH CHERRIES, ALMONDS & ORANGE BLOSSOM — p.16	TURKEY & VEGETABLE RAGÙ WITH TOMATOES, GARLIC & OREGANO — p.36	ALMOND MILK ICE CREAM WITH CRUSHED APRICOTS & CARDAMOM — p.52	SKILLET LAMB & COUSCOUS WITH CUMIN & RAISINS — p.66
Day 25	SPICED APPLE & DATE CRUMBLE WITH OLIVE OIL STREUSEL — p.43	MEDITERRANEAN MEATBALL TRAY WITH TOMATOES & CHICKPEAS — p.38	SEMIFREDDO WITH TOASTED ALMONDS & ORANGE RIBBONS — p.53	MEDITERRANEAN SHEPHERD'S PIE WITH GROUND BEEF & EGGPLANT — p.67
Day 26	SWEET POTATO AND EGG SKILLET WITH FETA AND DILL — p.20	ROASTED BEET SALAD WITH CHICKPEAS, DILL & LEMON YOGURT — p.39	GRILLED PEACHES WITH BASIL AND BALSAMIC REDUCTION — p.54	CREAMY POLENTA WITH ROASTED MUSHROOMS & GARLIC OIL — p.68
Day 27	SMASHED CHICKPEA & OLIVE TOAST WITH LEMON TAHINI DRIZZLE — p.20	GRILLED CHICKEN SALAD WITH QUINOA, FIGS & WALNUTS — p.41	WATERMELON WEDGES WITH FETA, MINT AND HONEY DRIZZLE — p.54	QUINOA & ROASTED CHICKEN BOWL WITH TAHINI DRESSING — p.69
Day 28	CREAMY POLENTA WITH POACHED EGG, OREGANO AND SPINACH — p.19	ORZO SALAD WITH TUNA, CHERRY TOMATOES & BASIL VINAIGRETTE — p.39	CARAMELIZED ORANGES WITH OLIVE OIL AND CINNAMON — p.55	PASTA WITH SARDINES, CAPERS & TOASTED BREADCRUMBS — p.69
Day 29	FARRO WITH CINNAMON APPLES AND CARDAMOM YOGURT — p.26	WHITE BEAN SALAD WITH SARDINES, ARUGULA & CAPERS — p.40	ROASTED APPLE RINGS WITH LABNEH AND ALMOND CRUST — p.56	BROCCOLI & CAULIFLOWER GRATIN WITH HERBED YOGURT DRIZZLE — p.71
Day 30	WARM OATS WITH ORANGE ZEST, DATES AND PISTACHIOS — p.24	LENTIL & TOMATO SALAD WITH FETA, OLIVES & FRESH THYME — p.42	PEAR AND PLUM SKILLET WITH CRUSHED WALNUTS AND OAT CRUST — p.57	CHICKEN THIGHS WITH ARTICHOKES, LEMON & BABY POTATOES — p.73

Your 30-Day Mediterranean Meal Plan

Healthy eating shouldn't feel complicated, overwhelming, or restrictive. The beauty of the Mediterranean lifestyle lies in its simplicity: fresh ingredients, vibrant flavors, and balanced meals that nourish your body and satisfy your soul.

This 30-Day Mediterranean Meal Plan is designed to make the transition effortless—whether you're new to this way of eating or simply looking for fresh inspiration. Every meal is thoughtfully crafted to be quick, flavorful, and aligned with the heart-healthy principles of the Mediterranean diet.

Here's what makes this meal plan different:

Every day features new, diverse recipes—no boring repetition

Balanced meals built around vegetables, lean proteins, healthy fats, and whole grains

Designed for real life—most recipes ready in 30 minutes or less

Family-friendly, adaptable for solo cooks, couples, or groups

Focused on seasonal, fresh ingredients for better taste and better health

This isn't a crash diet or a short-term fix—it's a roadmap to a healthier, more vibrant life. Over the course of 30 days, you'll discover how easy it is to fuel your body with nourishing food, boost your energy naturally, and fall in love with every bite.

With the help of this plan, you'll not only know what to eat each day but also how to bring variety and joy to your table—all while supporting heart health, balanced weight, and overall wellness.

Simple. Delicious. Sustainable. Let this plan be your guide to lasting Mediterranean success.

BREAKFAST: CHAPTER 2: Protein-Packed Mediterranean Mornings

ZA'ATAR-SPICED EGGS WITH SPINACH & SUMAC YOGURT

🔔 1 serving   🟢 15 min   🟢 Stovetop

INGREDIENTS:

2 large eggs (100g / ~3.5oz)
1 cup fresh spinach, chopped (30g / ~1oz)
2 tbsp plain Greek yogurt, 2% (30g / ~1oz)
1 tbsp extra virgin olive oil (15ml / ~0.5oz)
1/2 tsp za'atar spice blend (1g / ~0.04oz)

Also needed (not counted as main):
1/4 tsp sumac (0.5g / ~0.02oz)
1 garlic clove, grated (3g / ~0.1oz)
Salt and pepper to taste

INSTRUCTIONS:

1. In a small bowl, mix yogurt with sumac, garlic, and a pinch of sea salt. Set aside.
2. Heat olive oil in a skillet over medium. Add spinach and sauté for 1–2 minutes until wilted.
3. Push spinach to one side, crack in the eggs, and sprinkle with za'atar. Cook sunny-side up or to your liking.
4. Plate the spinach and eggs, top with the yogurt sauce, and season with black pepper.
5. Optional: garnish with extra za'atar or chili flakes.

■ Add a spoonful of hummus or sliced cucumber for a cooling touch.

> **Nutritional Information (Per Serving): Calories: 340 kcal | Protein: 18g | Fat: 15g | Carbs: 10g | Fiber: 6g | Net Carbs: 3g**

CHICKPEA HASH WITH ROASTED GARLIC AND FETA

🔔 1 serving   🟢 20 min   🟢 Stovetop

INGREDIENTS:

1/3 cup canned chickpeas, drained (80g / ~2.8oz)
1 large egg (50g / ~1.8oz)
1 oz crumbled feta cheese (28g / ~1oz)
1/2 small zucchini, diced (60g / ~2.1oz)
1 tbsp olive oil (15ml / ~0.5oz)

Also needed (not counted as main):
1 garlic clove, roasted and mashed (3g / ~0.1oz)
1/4 tsp smoked paprika (0.5g / ~0.02oz)
Fresh parsley for garnish
Salt and pepper to taste

INSTRUCTIONS:

1. Heat olive oil in a skillet over medium. Sauté zucchini for 3–4 minutes until soft and lightly browned.
2. Add chickpeas, roasted garlic, and paprika. Cook 2–3 minutes, stirring occasionally.
3. Make a well and crack in the egg. Cover and cook 3–4 minutes until white is set, yolk soft.
4. Top with feta, season, and cook uncovered for 1 minute. Garnish with parsley and serve warm.

■ To enhance flavor, add a squeeze of lemon juice just before serving.

> **Nutritional Information (Per Serving): Calories: 395 kcal | Protein: 17g | Fat: 16g | Carbs: 21g | Fiber: 7g | Net Carbs: 14g**

POACHED EGGS OVER WARM LENTILS & TOMATO CONFIT

🛎 1 serving   🟢 25 min   🌿 Stovetop

INGREDIENTS:

1/3 cup cooked green lentils (75g / ~2.6oz)
1 large egg (50g / ~1.8oz)
1/4 cup cherry tomatoes, halved (50g / ~1.8oz)
1/2 tbsp extra virgin olive oil (7ml / ~0.25oz)
1/2 tbsp red wine vinegar (7ml / ~0.25oz)

Also needed (not counted as main):
1/2 garlic clove, finely minced (1.5g / ~0.05oz)
1/4 tsp dried thyme (0.5g / ~0.02oz)
Fresh parsley, chopped, for garnish
Salt and pepper to taste

INSTRUCTIONS:

1. Heat olive oil in a skillet over medium. Add garlic and cook for 30 seconds.
2. Add cherry tomatoes and thyme. Cook uncovered for 5–6 minutes until soft and jammy.
3. Stir in lentils and vinegar. Season with salt and pepper. Simmer for 2–3 minutes to warm through.
4. Meanwhile, poach the egg in simmering water for 3–4 minutes until white is set and yolk is soft.
5. Transfer lentils to a bowl, top with the poached egg, garnish with parsley, and serve warm.

▪ Use pre-cooked lentils to save time; refrigerate leftovers for up to 3 days.

Nutritional Information (Per Serving): **Calories: 370 kcal | Protein: 18g | Fat: 13g | Carbs: 24g | Fiber: 7g | Net Carbs: 17g**

HERB OMELETTE WITH SUNDRIED TOMATOES & OLIVE TAPENADE

🛎 1 serving   🟢 15 min   🌿 Stovetop

INGREDIENTS:

2 large eggs (100g / ~3.5oz)
1 tbsp chopped sun-dried tomatoes, drained (10g / ~0.35oz)
1 tbsp olive tapenade (15g / ~0.5oz)
1/2 tbsp chopped fresh parsley (2g / ~0.07oz)
1/2 tbsp olive oil (7ml / ~0.25oz)

Also needed (not counted as main):
1/2 tbsp water (7ml / ~0.25oz)
Salt and black pepper to taste

INSTRUCTIONS:

1. Whisk eggs with water, parsley, salt, and pepper until frothy.
2. Heat olive oil in a nonstick skillet over medium. Pour in eggs and swirl to coat the pan.
3. Cook for 1–2 minutes until the edges begin to set. Lift gently to let uncooked egg flow underneath.
4. When nearly set, add sun-dried tomatoes and tapenade to one side.
5. Fold the omelette and cook for another 1–2 minutes until just set. Serve hot, garnished with parsley if desired.

▪ Pairs well with arugula or sliced cucumbers for a refreshing contrast.

Nutritional Information (Per Serving): **Calories: 355 kcal | Protein: 19g | Fat: 15g | Carbs: 10g | Fiber: 6g | Net Carbs: 3g**

SMOKED SALMON WITH AVOCADO LABNEH AND DILL CRUNCH

🔔 1 serving   🟢 10 min   🌿 No cook

INGREDIENTS:

2 oz smoked salmon, thinly sliced (56g)
3 tbsp labneh (45g / 1.6oz)
1/2 small avocado, mashed (70g / 2.5oz)
1 tbsp fresh dill, chopped (2g / 0.07oz)
1 tbsp chopped cucumber (15g / 0.5oz)

Also needed (not counted as main):
1/2 tsp lemon juice (2ml / 0.07oz)
1/2 tsp extra virgin olive oil (2.5ml / 0.08oz)
Salt and black pepper to taste

INSTRUCTIONS:

1. In a small bowl, mix labneh with mashed avocado, lemon juice, and a pinch of salt.
2. Spread the avocado-labneh blend on a plate or toast (if desired).
3. Layer smoked salmon on top and sprinkle with chopped dill and cucumber.
4. Drizzle with olive oil, crack fresh pepper over the top, and serve chilled or at room temperature.

▪ *Swap dill with chives or parsley for a different herbal profile.*

Nutritional Information (Per Serving): **Calories: 340 kcal | Protein: 18g | Fat: 16g | Carbs: 10g | Fiber: 6g | Net Carbs: 4g**

TURKEY AND CHICKPEA BREAKFAST SKILLET WITH LEMON OIL

🔔 1 serving   🟢 20 min   🌿 Stovetop

INGREDIENTS:

3 oz ground turkey, lean (85g)
1/4 cup cooked chickpeas, rinsed (60g / 2.1oz)
1/4 small red onion, sliced (25g / 0.9oz)
1/4 cup cherry tomatoes, halved (40g / 1.4oz)
1 tbsp chopped flat-leaf parsley (2g / 0.07oz)

Also needed (not counted as main):
1 tsp lemon zest (2g / 0.07oz)
1 tsp extra virgin olive oil (5ml / 0.17oz)
1 garlic clove, minced (3g / 0.1oz)
Sea salt and pepper to taste

INSTRUCTIONS:

1. Heat olive oil in a skillet over medium. Add garlic and onion, sauté 2–3 min until soft.
2. Add ground turkey, breaking it up with a spatula, and cook until browned (5–6 min).
3. Stir in chickpeas and cherry tomatoes. Cook another 5 minutes, until tomatoes soften.
4. Sprinkle with lemon zest, parsley, and season to taste.

▪ *For extra fiber, stir in a handful of spinach in the last 2 minutes of cooking.*

Nutritional Information (Per Serving): **Calories: 395 kcal | Protein: 20g | Fat: 14g | Carbs: 22g | Fiber: 7g | Net Carbs: 15g**

EGG WHITE FRITTATA WITH ROASTED ZUCCHINI AND PESTO

🔔 1 serving   ● 20 min   ● Oven

INGREDIENTS:

4 large egg whites (130g / 4.6oz)
1/2 small zucchini, diced (80g / 2.8oz)
1 tbsp basil pesto (15g / 0.5oz)
2 tbsp grated Parmesan (15g / 0.5oz)
1 tsp olive oil (5ml / 0.17oz)

Also needed (not counted as main):
1 tbsp chopped scallions (8g / 0.3oz)
Salt and black pepper to taste

INSTRUCTIONS:

1. Preheat oven to 375°F (190°C). Line a small baking dish or oven-safe skillet with parchment or lightly oil it.
2. Toss diced zucchini with olive oil, salt, and pepper. Roast in the oven for 10 minutes or until lightly browned.
3. In a bowl, whisk egg whites with Parmesan, scallions, a pinch of salt, and black pepper until slightly frothy.
4. Pour the egg white mixture into the prepared dish. Gently scatter roasted zucchini on top and spoon small dollops of pesto evenly across.
5. Bake for 10–12 minutes until the frittata is set in the center and slightly golden around the edges. Let cool for 1 minute before serving warm.

▪ *Try using arugula pesto for a peppery twist.*

> **Nutritional Information (Per Serving): Calories: 335 kcal | Protein: 19g | Fat: 14g | Carbs: 12g | Fiber: 6g | Net Carbs: 6g**

SAVORY COTTAGE CHEESE BOWL WITH GRILLED ASPARAGUS AND CAPERS

🔔 1 serving   ● 15 min   ● Stovetop

INGREDIENTS:

1/2 cup low-fat cottage cheese (115g / 4oz)
5 spears asparagus, trimmed (75g / 2.6oz)
1 tsp capers, rinsed (5g / 0.18oz)
1 tsp olive oil (5ml / 0.17oz)
1 tbsp chopped fresh dill (2g / 0.07oz)

Also needed (not counted as main):
1/2 tsp lemon zest (1g / 0.04oz)
Salt and black pepper to taste

INSTRUCTIONS:

1. Heat olive oil in a nonstick skillet over medium heat. Add asparagus and cook for 4–5 minutes, turning occasionally, until tender and lightly charred.
2. Spoon cottage cheese into a serving bowl and season lightly with salt and pepper.
3. Arrange grilled asparagus on top. Sprinkle with capers, fresh dill, and lemon zest.
4. Drizzle a few extra drops of olive oil over the top if desired and serve immediately.

▪ *For extra crunch, add a few pumpkin seeds or toasted almonds on top.*

> **Nutritional Information (Per Serving): Calories: 345 kcal | Protein: 17g | Fat: 13g | Carbs: 14g | Fiber: 7g | Net Carbs: 7g**

CHAPTER 3: Whole Grains with a Twist

WARM FARRO WITH CHERRIES, ALMONDS & ORANGE BLOSSOM

🔔 1 serving ● 25 min ● Stove + simmer

INGREDIENTS:

1/3 cup farro (50g / 1.75oz)
1/2 cup low-fat milk (120ml / 4oz)
3 tbsp cherries, fresh or dried (25g / 0.9oz)
1 tbsp sliced almonds (8g / 0.28oz)
1 tsp low-carb sweetener or honey (5ml / 0.17oz)
1/2 tsp orange blossom water (2.5ml / 0.08oz)

Also needed (not counted as main):
Pinch of salt
Optional: pinch of cinnamon or vanilla extract for aroma

INSTRUCTIONS:

1. Rinse farro. In a small saucepan, combine farro, milk, and a pinch of salt. Bring to a boil.
2. Lower heat to simmer, cover and cook for 15–18 min until milk is mostly absorbed.
3. Stir in cherries, orange blossom water, and sweetener. Let warm for another 2 min.
4. Transfer to a bowl and sprinkle with sliced almonds.

■ Swap dried cherries for fresh berries or chopped dates for a different flavor profile.

> *Nutritional Information (Per Serving):* **Calories: 350 kcal** | Protein: 17g | Fat: 13g | Carbs: 30g | Fiber: 7g | Net Carbs: 23g

MILLET & OLIVE BREAKFAST CAKES WITH FETA CRUMBLE

🔔 1 serving ● 30 min ● Stove

INGREDIENTS:

1/4 cup millet (50g / 1.75oz)
1/2 cup water (120ml / 4oz)
1 tbsp chopped green olives (15g / 0.5oz)
1 tbsp crumbled feta (15g / 0.5oz)
1 small egg (40g / 1.4oz)
2 tsp olive oil (10ml / 0.34oz)

Also needed (not counted as main):
Salt and pepper to taste
¼ tsp dried oregano (0.5g / ~0.02oz)

INSTRUCTIONS:

1. Rinse millet. In a small pot, bring water to boil. Add millet, lower heat, and simmer 12–15 min until soft and water is absorbed. Let cool slightly.
2. Mix millet with chopped olives, egg, oregano, salt, and pepper. Form a thick patty.
3. Heat oil in a pan over medium heat. Fry patty for 4–5 min per side until golden and crisp.
4. Serve warm topped with crumbled feta.

■ Add chopped spinach or herbs into the batter for extra fiber and color.

> *Nutritional Information (Per Serving):* **Calories: 370 kcal** | Protein: 18g | Fat: 14g | Carbs: 28g | Fiber: 6g | Net Carbs: 22g

BARLEY BOWL WITH ROASTED APPLES & THYME YOGURT

🔔 1 serving   ⬤ 25 min   ⬤ Oven + stove

INGREDIENTS:

1/4 cup pearl barley (50g / 1.75oz)
1/2 cup low-fat Greek yogurt (120g / 4.2oz)
1/2 medium apple, sliced (70g / 2.5oz)
1/2 tbsp olive oil (7ml / 0.24oz)
1 tsp low-carb sweetener (5ml / 0.17oz)
1/2 tsp fresh thyme leaves (0.5g / 0.02oz)

Also needed (not counted as main):
Salt and black pepper to taste
Optional: a squeeze of lemon juice over apples before roasting

INSTRUCTIONS:

1. Preheat oven to 400°F (200°C).
2. Cook barley in 1 cup water until tender, 18–20 min.
3. Toss apple slices with olive oil and thyme. Roast on baking sheet for 12–15 min.
4. Mix yogurt with sweetener and a pinch of salt.
5. Assemble bowl: barley on bottom, top with warm roasted apples and thyme yogurt. Serve warm or chilled.

▌*Separately For Avocado Mayo:* Use cinnamon instead of thyme for a sweet twist or add chopped walnuts for crunch.

> *Nutritional Information (Per Serving):* **Calories: 360 kcal | Protein: 17g | Fat: 13g | Carbs: 30g | Fiber: 7g | Net Carbs: 23g**

SAVORY QUINOA PORRIDGE WITH CARROT, TAHINI & CHIVES

🔔 1 serving   ⬤ 25 min   ⬤ Stove

INGREDIENTS:

1/4 cup quinoa (45g / 1.6oz)
1/2 cup water (120ml / 4oz)
1/2 small carrot, grated (30g / 1oz)
1 tbsp tahini (15g / 0.5oz)
1 tbsp chopped chives (4g / 0.14oz)
1 large egg (50g / 1.8oz)
1/2 tbsp olive oil (7ml / 0.24oz)

Also needed (not counted as main):
Salt and pepper to taste
Optional: chili flakes or lemon zest

INSTRUCTIONS:

1. Rinse quinoa, cook with water over low heat for 12–15 min until soft.
2. In small pan, heat olive oil and quickly sauté grated carrot for 2 min.
3. Stir carrot into quinoa along with tahini and half of the chives.
4. Fry or poach the egg to your liking.
5. Spoon porridge into a bowl, top with egg and remaining chives. Season to taste.

▌*Top with extra tahini drizzle or add baby spinach for extra greens.*

> *Nutritional Information (Per Serving):* **Calories: 375 kcal | Protein: 18g | Fat: 15g | Carbs: 28g | Fiber: 6g | Net Carbs: 22g**

COUSCOUS WITH ROASTED PEPPERS, OLIVES & SOFT EGG

🔔 1 serving ● 20 min 🌿 Stove + roast

INGREDIENTS:

1/4 cup whole wheat couscous (40g / 1.4oz)
1 medium egg (50g / 1.8oz)
1/4 cup roasted red pepper, chopped (40g / 1.4oz)
1 tbsp sliced green or Kalamata olives (15g / 0.5oz)
1 tbsp olive oil (15ml / 0.5oz)

Also needed (not counted as main):
Salt and pepper to taste
½ tsp lemon juice (2.5ml / ~0.08oz)
Optional: chopped parsley or mint to garnish

INSTRUCTIONS:

1. Place couscous in a bowl. Add ⅓ cup boiling water and cover. Let sit 5 min, fluff with fork.
2. While couscous sits, roast or pan-fry red pepper slices for 5 min until slightly charred.
3. Soft-boil egg for 6 min, then peel.
4. Toss couscous with olive oil, lemon juice, olives, roasted pepper, salt and pepper.
5. Top with halved soft egg and fresh herbs.

■ *Swap in sun-dried tomatoes for extra umami, or add arugula for greens.*

> *Nutritional Information (Per Serving):* **Calories: 370 kcal | Protein: 17g | Fat: 14g | Carbs: 29g | Fiber: 7g | Net Carbs: 22g**

SPICED FREEKEH WITH PISTACHIOS & LABNEH SWIRL

🔔 1 serving ● 25 min 🌿 Stove

INGREDIENTS:

1/4 cup freekeh (50g / 1.75oz)
1 tbsp shelled pistachios, chopped (12g / 0.4oz)
2 tbsp labneh or thick Greek yogurt (30g / 1oz)
1/2 tbsp olive oil (7ml / 0.24oz)
1/4 tsp ground cumin (0.5g / 0.02oz)

Also needed (not counted as main):
Salt to taste
Optional: pinch of smoked paprika or fresh lemon zest

INSTRUCTIONS:

1. Rinse freekeh. Cook in ⅔ cup water with pinch of salt for 18–20 min until tender.
2. Stir in olive oil, cumin, and paprika if using. Let stand covered 2 min.
3. Spoon into a bowl, swirl in labneh, sprinkle with chopped pistachios.
4. Garnish with lemon zest or fresh herbs if desired. Serve warm.

■ ***For homemade tapenade:***
Use za'atar or fresh thyme for added complexity. Sub labneh with cottage cheese for higher protein.

> *Nutritional Information (Per Serving):* **Calories: 390 kcal | Protein: 18g | Fat: 15g | Carbs: 28g | Fiber: 7g | Net Carbs: 21g**

BAKED BULGUR PATTIES WITH TOMATO-MINT CHUTNEY

🔔 1 serving • 🟢 25 min • 🟢 Oven

INGREDIENTS:

1/4 cup fine bulgur, dry (40g / ~1.4oz)
1 small egg (50g / ~1.8oz)
2 tbsp crumbled feta cheese (28g / ~1oz)
1 tbsp chopped fresh parsley (4g / ~0.14oz)
1 tbsp olive oil (15ml / ~0.5oz)

For Tomato-Mint Chutney:
1/3 cup cherry tomatoes, finely chopped (50g / ~1.8oz)
1 tsp chopped fresh mint (2g / ~0.07oz)
1/2 tsp red wine vinegar (2.5ml / ~0.08oz)
Salt and pepper to taste

INSTRUCTIONS:

1. Preheat oven to 375°F (190°C).
2. In a bowl, soak bulgur in hot water for 10 min, then drain and squeeze dry.
3. Mix bulgur with egg, feta, parsley, and a pinch of salt and pepper.
4. Shape into 2–3 small patties and place on a lined baking tray. Drizzle with olive oil.
5. Bake for 12–15 min, flipping halfway, until golden and firm.
6. Meanwhile, combine cherry tomatoes, mint, vinegar, and a pinch of salt in a small bowl. Let sit to meld flavors.
7. Serve the warm patties with a spoonful of tomato-mint chutney on top.

■ Add a dash of cumin to the patties for extra depth.

Nutritional Information (Per Serving): **Calories: 370 kcal | Protein: 17g | Fat: 14g | Carbs: 26g | Fiber: 7g | Net Carbs: 19g**

CREAMY POLENTA WITH POACHED EGG, OREGANO AND SPINACH

🔔 1 serving • 🟢 20 min • 🟢 Stovetop

INGREDIENTS:

1/4 cup instant polenta (35g / ~1.2oz)
1 poached egg (50g / ~1.8oz)
1/2 cup cooked spinach, drained (60g / ~2.1oz)
1 tbsp grated Parmesan cheese (7g / ~0.25oz)
1 tbsp olive oil (15ml / ~0.5oz)

Also needed (not counted as main):
1 cup water or low-sodium vegetable broth (240ml / ~8oz)
1/4 tsp dried oregano (0.5g / ~0.02oz)
Salt and pepper to taste

INSTRUCTIONS:

1. In a saucepan, bring water or broth to a simmer. Slowly whisk in polenta.
2. Cook over low heat, stirring for 4–5 min until creamy. Stir in Parmesan and half the olive oil.
3. Sauté spinach with remaining olive oil and oregano until just wilted.
4. Poach the egg in simmering water with a splash of vinegar for 3–4 min until whites are set.
5. Spoon polenta into a bowl, top with spinach and poached egg.

■ Add a squeeze of lemon over the spinach for a fresh lift.

Nutritional Information (Per Serving): **Calories: 395 kcal | Protein: 16g | Fat: 15g | Carbs: 28g | Fiber: 6g | Net Carbs: 22g**

CHAPTER 4: Baked & Skillet Delights

SMASHED CHICKPEA & OLIVE TOAST WITH LEMON TAHINI DRIZZLE

🔔 1 serving   🟢 15 min   🟢 Stovetop, No-Bake

INGREDIENTS:

1/3 cup canned chickpeas, rinsed and drained (60g / ~2.1oz)
1 slice whole grain bread, toasted (35g / ~1.2oz)
1 tbsp chopped Kalamata olives (10g / ~0.35oz)
1 tbsp tahini (15g / ~0.5oz)
1 tsp lemon juice (5ml / ~0.17oz)

Also needed (not counted as main):
1/4 tsp cumin (0.5g / ~0.02oz), optional
Salt and pepper to taste
1 tbsp water (15ml / ~0.5oz) to thin tahini

INSTRUCTIONS:

1. In a bowl, lightly mash chickpeas with a fork. Stir in olives, cumin, salt, and pepper.
2. In a small dish, whisk tahini with lemon juice and water until smooth and pourable.
3. Toast the bread until golden, then top with the chickpea mixture.
4. Drizzle generously with lemon tahini sauce and serve immediately.

◼ *Add fresh parsley or crushed red pepper for a punch of color and spice.*

> *Nutritional Information (Per Serving):* **Calories: 345 kcal | Protein: 16g | Fat: 14g | Carbs: 28g | Fiber: 7g | Net Carbs: 21g**

SWEET POTATO AND EGG SKILLET WITH FETA AND DILL

🔔 1 serving   🟢 20 min   🟢 Stovetop

INGREDIENTS:

1/2 small sweet potato, diced (80g / ~2.8oz)
1 large egg (50g / ~1.8oz)
1 tbsp crumbled feta cheese (14g / ~0.5oz)
1 tbsp chopped fresh dill (3g / ~0.1oz)
1 tbsp olive oil (15ml / ~0.5oz)

Also needed (not counted as main):
Salt and black pepper to taste
Optional: 2 tbsp diced red onion (20g / ~0.7oz)

INSTRUCTIONS:

1. Heat olive oil in a skillet over medium heat. Add diced sweet potato and cook 8–10 min until golden and tender, stirring occasionally.
2. Add red onion if using and cook 2 min more.
3. Push potatoes to one side. Crack in egg and cover the skillet. Cook 3–4 min until the egg white is set but yolk is soft.
4. Sprinkle with feta, dill, salt, and pepper. Serve hot in the skillet or on a plate.

◼ *Tip: For extra flavor, finish with a splash of lemon juice or pinch of smoked paprika.*

> *Nutritional Information (Per Serving):* **Calories: 390 kcal | Protein: 17g | Fat: 15g | Carbs: 27g | Fiber: 6g | Net Carbs: 21g**

TOMATO & GOAT CHEESE GALETTE WITH THYME SEED CRUST

🔔 1 serving   🟢 25 min   🟢 Oven

INGREDIENTS:

1/4 cup almond flour (25g / ~0.9oz)
1 tbsp ground flaxseed (7g / ~0.25oz)
1 tbsp olive oil (15ml / ~0.5oz)
2 tbsp soft goat cheese (30g / ~1oz)
1/3 cup sliced cherry tomatoes (50g / ~1.8oz)

Also needed (not counted as main):
1/2 tsp chopped fresh thyme (1g / ~0.04oz)
1 tsp water (5ml / ~0.17oz)
Salt and black pepper to taste

INSTRUCTIONS:

1. Preheat oven to 375°F (190°C).
2. In a bowl, mix almond flour, flaxseed, thyme, olive oil, and water. Press dough into a 4–5 inch (10–12cm) round on parchment paper.
3. Spread goat cheese in the center, leaving a 1/2-inch (1cm) border. Top with sliced tomatoes, salt, and pepper.
4. Fold edges gently over the filling. Bake 15–18 min until golden and crisp.
5. Let cool 2 min before serving.

▪ Add a few basil leaves or a drizzle of balsamic for extra depth.

Nutritional Information (Per Serving): **Calories: 385 kcal | Protein: 16g | Fat: 15g | Carbs: 14g | Fiber: 7g | Net Carbs: 7g**

ZUCCHINI PANCAKES WITH YOGURT-DILL SAUCE AND PINE NUTS

🔔 1 serving   🟢 20 min   🟢 Stovetop

INGREDIENTS:

1/2 medium zucchini, grated and squeezed (80g / ~2.8oz)
1 large egg (50g / ~1.8oz)
1 tbsp whole-milk plain yogurt (15g / ~0.5oz)
1 tbsp crumbled feta (14g / ~0.5oz)
1 tsp pine nuts, toasted (5g / ~0.18oz)

Also needed (not counted as main):
1/2 tbsp olive oil (7ml / ~0.25oz)
1/2 tsp chopped fresh dill (1g / ~0.04oz)
Salt and pepper to taste

INSTRUCTIONS:

1. In a bowl, mix zucchini, egg, feta, salt, and pepper. Form into 2–3 small pancakes.
2. Heat olive oil in a skillet over medium heat. Cook pancakes 3–4 min per side until golden and firm.
3. In a small bowl, mix yogurt with dill.
4. Serve warm pancakes topped with yogurt-dill sauce and sprinkle with pine nuts.

▪ For a crispier texture, add 1 tsp chickpea flour to the mix.

Nutritional Information (Per Serving): **Calories: 370 kcal | Protein: 17g | Fat: 14g | Carbs: 16g | Fiber: 6g | Net Carbs: 10g**

BAKED EGGS IN EGGPLANT CUPS WITH PARSLEY PESTO

🔔 1 serving   ● 25 min   ● Oven

INGREDIENTS:

1 small eggplant, halved lengthwise (150g / ~5.3oz)
1 large egg (50g / ~1.8oz)
1 tbsp grated Parmesan cheese (7g / ~0.25oz)
1 tbsp olive oil (15ml / ~0.5oz)
1 tbsp fresh parsley pesto (15g / ~0.5oz)

Also needed (not counted as main):
Salt and black pepper to taste
Optional: 1 tsp lemon juice (5ml / ~0.17oz)

INSTRUCTIONS:

1. Preheat oven to 375°F (190°C). Scoop out some flesh from each eggplant half to form shallow "cups."
2. Brush inside with olive oil and bake cut-side up for 10 min until tender.
3. Remove tray, carefully crack an egg into each cup. Sprinkle with Parmesan.
4. Return to oven and bake for 10–12 min, or until egg white is just set and yolk still soft.
5. Top with parsley pesto and season with salt, pepper, and a squeeze of lemon if using.

■ You can blend parsley, olive oil, garlic, and nuts to make a quick homemade pesto.

Nutritional Information (Per Serving): **Calories: 385 kcal | Protein: 18g | Fat: 15g | Carbs: 20g | Fiber: 7g | Net Carbs: 13g**

MUSHROOM & RED ONION TARTLETS WITH CRUMBLED FETA

🔔 1 serving   ● 30 min   ● Oven

INGREDIENTS:

1/4 cup sliced mushrooms (50g / ~1.8oz)
2 tbsp chopped red onion (20g / ~0.7oz)
1 tbsp crumbled feta cheese (14g / ~0.5oz)
1/4 cup almond flour (25g / ~0.9oz)
1 tbsp olive oil (15ml / ~0.5oz)

Also needed (not counted as main):
1 small egg (50g / ~1.8oz)
1/4 tsp dried oregano (0.5g / ~0.02oz)
Salt and pepper to taste

INSTRUCTIONS:

1. Preheat oven to 375°F (190°C). Grease a ramekin or tartlet pan.
2. In a bowl, mix almond flour with half the olive oil and a pinch of salt. Press into the base of the pan to form a crust.
3. Bake crust for 8 min until lightly golden. Meanwhile, sauté mushrooms and onion in remaining oil for 5–6 min.
4. In another bowl, beat egg with oregano, salt, and pepper. Stir in cooked veggies.
5. Pour filling over crust, top with crumbled feta, and bake for 10–12 min until set. Let cool slightly and serve.

■ Try adding chopped spinach or thyme for variation.

Nutritional Information (Per Serving): **Calories: 395 kcal | Protein: 17g | Fat: 16g | Carbs: 14g | Fiber: 6g | Net Carbs: 8g**

CHAPTER 5: Naturally Sweet Starts

BAKED PEAR WITH RICOTTA, HONEY & TOASTED WALNUTS

🔔 1 serving   🟢 20 min   🌿 Oven

INGREDIENTS:

1 medium ripe pear, halved and cored (150g / ~5.3oz)
1/4 cup ricotta cheese (60g / ~2.1oz)
1 tbsp chopped walnuts, toasted (8g / ~0.3oz)
1 tsp honey (7g / ~0.25oz)
1/2 tsp olive oil (2.5ml / ~0.08oz)

Also needed (not counted as main):
1/4 tsp cinnamon (0.5g / ~0.02oz)
Optional: pinch of sea salt or lemon zest

INSTRUCTIONS:

1. Preheat oven to 375°F (190°C). Place pear halves cut-side up in a small baking dish and brush with olive oil.
2. Bake for 10–12 min until soft and lightly caramelized.
3. While baking, toast walnuts in a dry pan over low heat for 2–3 min until fragrant.
4. Remove pears from oven, spoon ricotta into the center of each half, and drizzle with honey.
5. Sprinkle with cinnamon, walnuts, and optional lemon zest.

▪ *You can swap honey for a few drops of low carb sweetener to reduce sugar.*

> ***Nutritional Information (Per Serving):* Calories: 360 kcal | Protein: 16g | Fat: 14g | Carbs: 28g | Fiber: 7g | Net Carbs: 21g**

FIG AND HAZELNUT BREAKFAST CLUSTERS WITH YOGURT CREAM

🔔 1 serving   🟢 25 min   🌿 Oven

INGREDIENTS:

2 dried figs, chopped (30g / ~1oz)
2 tbsp chopped hazelnuts (16g / ~0.56oz)
1 tbsp rolled oats (8g / ~0.28oz)
1/2 tbsp olive oil (7ml / ~0.25oz)
1/3 cup plain Greek yogurt (75g / ~2.6oz)

Also needed (not counted as main):
1/4 tsp cinnamon (0.5g / ~0.02oz)
1/2 tsp low carb sweetener (2g / ~0.07oz), optional
Pinch of salt

INSTRUCTIONS:

1. Preheat oven to 350°F (175°C). Line a small tray with parchment.
2. Mix chopped figs, hazelnuts, oats, olive oil, cinnamon, and a pinch of salt in a bowl. Shape into small clusters and place on tray.
3. Bake for 10–12 min until golden. Let cool fully so they firm up.
4. Stir yogurt with low carb sweetener if using.
5. Serve clusters over the yogurt or on the side for dipping.

▪ *For extra protein, add a spoonful of whey or plant protein to the yogurt.*

> ***Nutritional Information (Per Serving):* Calories: 375 kcal | Protein: 17g | Fat: 15g | Carbs: 24g | Fiber: 8g | Net Carbs: 16g**

WARM OATS WITH ORANGE ZEST, DATES AND PISTACHIOS

🔔 1 serving ● 15 min ● Stovetop

INGREDIENTS:

1/4 cup rolled oats (20g / ~0.7oz)
1/2 cup unsweetened soy milk (120ml / ~4.2oz)
1 tbsp chopped Medjool dates (15g / ~0.5oz)
1 tbsp chopped pistachios (10g / ~0.35oz)
1/4 cup plain Greek yogurt (60g / ~2.1oz)

Also needed (not counted as main):
1/2 tsp orange zest (1g / ~0.04oz)
Optional: pinch of cinnamon or low carb sweetener

INSTRUCTIONS:

1. In a small saucepan, bring soy milk to a gentle simmer over medium heat.
2. Stir in rolled oats and cook, stirring occasionally, for 5–6 min until creamy.
3. Add chopped dates and orange zest. Stir well and let sit for 1 min off heat.
4. Transfer oats to a bowl. Top with Greek yogurt and chopped pistachios.
5. Sprinkle with cinnamon or low carb sweetener if using.

▌ You can prep the oats the night before and simply reheat in the morning.

Nutritional Information (Per Serving): **Calories: 370 kcal | Protein: 18g | Fat: 14g | Carbs: 27g | Fiber: 7g | Net Carbs: 20g**

COUSCOUS BREAKFAST BOWL WITH APRICOTS & ROSE WATER

🔔 1 serving ● 20 min ● Stovetop

INGREDIENTS:

1/4 cup whole wheat couscous (40g / ~1.4oz)
1/3 cup boiling water (80ml / ~2.8oz)
2 dried apricots, finely chopped (20g / ~0.7oz)
1/4 cup low-fat ricotta cheese (60g / ~2.1oz)
1 tsp chopped almonds (5g / ~0.18oz)

Also needed (not counted as main):
1/4 tsp rose water (1.25ml / ~0.04oz), optional
Pinch of cinnamon or cardamom

INSTRUCTIONS:

1. In a small bowl, combine couscous and chopped apricots.
2. Pour boiling water over the mixture, cover with a lid or plate, and let steam for 5–6 min.
3. Fluff couscous with a fork and stir in rose water, if using.
4. Spoon into a serving bowl. Add ricotta on top and sprinkle with almonds.
5. Dust with cinnamon or cardamom. Serve warm or at room temperature.

▌ For extra texture, toast the almonds briefly in a dry skillet before adding.

Nutritional Information (Per Serving): **Calories: 385 kcal | Protein: 17g | Fat: 13g | Carbs: 28g | Fiber: 6g | Net Carbs: 22g**

ROASTED GRAPES WITH LABNEH AND ALMOND CRUNCH

🔔 1 serving ⏱ 20 min 🔥 Oven

INGREDIENTS:

1/2 cup red seedless grapes (75g / ~2.6oz)
1/4 cup labneh (60g / ~2.1oz)
1 tbsp chopped almonds, toasted (10g / ~0.35oz)
1/2 tsp olive oil (2.5ml / ~0.08oz)
1/4 tsp fresh rosemary, finely chopped (0.5g / ~0.02oz)

Also needed (not counted as main):
Pinch of sea salt and black pepper
Optional: 1/2 tsp low carb sweetener (2g / ~0.07oz)

INSTRUCTIONS:

1. Preheat oven to 375°F (190°C). Toss grapes with olive oil, rosemary, salt, and pepper.
2. Spread grapes on a parchment-lined tray and roast for 12–15 min, until soft and slightly blistered.
3. Spoon labneh into a shallow bowl. Top with warm grapes and sprinkle with toasted almonds.
4. Drizzle with a few drops of olive oil and add sweetener if desired.

▪ *Use Greek yogurt if labneh is unavailable, but drain it slightly for thickness.*

> *Nutritional Information (Per Serving):* **Calories: 365 kcal | Protein: 17g | Fat: 14g | Carbs: 24g | Fiber: 6g | Net Carbs: 18g**

CREAMY MILLET WITH BERRIES, CHIA, AND MINT SYRUP

🔔 1 serving ⏱ 25 min 🔥 Stovetop

INGREDIENTS:

1/4 cup cooked millet (50g / ~1.8oz)
1/4 cup mixed berries, fresh or thawed (50g / ~1.8oz)
1/2 cup unsweetened almond milk (120ml / ~4.2oz)
1 tbsp plain Greek yogurt (15g / ~0.5oz)
1 tsp chia seeds (5g / ~0.18oz)

Also needed (not counted as main):
1 tsp finely chopped fresh mint (2g / ~0.07oz)
1/2 tsp low carb sweetener (2g / ~0.07oz), optional

INSTRUCTIONS:

1. In a small saucepan, combine cooked millet and almond milk. Simmer over low heat for 5–6 min, stirring often, until creamy.
2. Stir in chia seeds and cook 2 min more until thickened.
3. In a small cup, mix sweetener with chopped mint and 1 tsp warm water to make a light syrup.
4. Pour millet into a bowl. Top with yogurt, berries, and drizzle with mint syrup.

▪ *Cook millet in advance and store chilled for quick breakfasts all week.*

> *Nutritional Information (Per Serving):* **Calories: 380 kcal | Protein: 16g | Fat: 13g | Carbs: 25g | Fiber: 7g | Net Carbs: 18g**

FARRO WITH CINNAMON APPLES AND CARDAMOM YOGURT

🔔 1 serving ● 25 min ● Stovetop

INGREDIENTS:

1/4 cup cooked farro (50g / ~1.8oz)
1/2 small apple, diced (60g / ~2.1oz)
1/3 cup plain Greek yogurt (80g / ~2.8oz)
1 tsp chopped walnuts (5g / ~0.18oz)
1/2 tsp olive oil (2.5ml / ~0.08oz)

Also needed (not counted as main):
1/4 tsp ground cinnamon (0.5g / ~0.02oz)
1/8 tsp ground cardamom (0.2g / ~0.007oz)
Optional: 1/2 tsp low carb sweetener (2g / ~0.07oz)

INSTRUCTIONS:

1. In a skillet, heat olive oil and sauté diced apple with cinnamon for 4–5 min until soft and lightly golden.
2. Warm the cooked farro briefly in a pan or microwave, then spoon into a bowl.
3. Top with the sautéed apples and chopped walnuts.
4. In a separate bowl, stir cardamom (and sweetener if using) into yogurt.
5. Spoon yogurt over the warm bowl and serve immediately.

■ *Farro can be pre-cooked and stored chilled for up to 3 days.*

> *Nutritional Information (Per Serving):* **Calories: 370 kcal | Protein: 17g | Fat: 13g | Carbs: 26g | Fiber: 7g | Net Carbs: 19g**

OAT YOGURT PARFAIT WITH PLUMS AND POMEGRANATE MOLASSES

🔔 1 serving ● 20 min ● No cook

INGREDIENTS:

1/4 cup rolled oats (20g / ~0.7oz)
1/2 ripe plum, sliced (50g / ~1.8oz)
1/3 cup plain Greek yogurt (80g / ~2.8oz)
1 tsp pomegranate molasses (5ml / ~0.17oz)
1 tsp chopped pistachios (5g / ~0.18oz)

Also needed (not counted as main):
1/4 tsp ground cinnamon (0.5g / ~0.02oz)
Optional: 1/2 tsp low carb sweetener (2g / ~0.07oz)

INSTRUCTIONS:

1. In a bowl, combine oats with 2 tbsp water and let sit for 10 min to soften.
2. In a serving glass or bowl, layer softened oats, yogurt, and sliced plums.
3. Drizzle with pomegranate molasses and sprinkle with pistachios and cinnamon.
4. Add sweetener if desired. Serve chilled or at room temperature.

■ *For extra creaminess, mix oats directly into the yogurt before layering.*

> *Nutritional Information (Per Serving):* **Calories: 360 kcal | Protein: 16g | Fat: 12g | Carbs: 25g | Fiber: 6g | Net Carbs: 19g**

LUNCH: CHAPTER 6: Hearty Bowls & Grain-Based Lunches

WARM COUSCOUS BOWL WITH HARISSA CHICKPEAS, SPINACH & FETA

🔔 1 serving   🟢 25 min   🟢 Stovetop

INGREDIENTS:

1/4 cup whole wheat couscous, dry (40g / ~1.4oz)
1/3 cup canned chickpeas, drained (60g / ~2.1oz)
1 cup baby spinach (30g / ~1oz)
2 tbsp crumbled feta cheese (30g / ~1oz)
1 tbsp olive oil (15ml / ~0.5oz)

Also needed (not counted as main):
1 tsp harissa paste (5g / ~0.17oz)
1/2 tsp lemon juice (2.5ml / ~0.08oz)
Salt and pepper to taste

INSTRUCTIONS:

1. In a heatproof bowl, pour 1/3 cup (80ml) boiling water over couscous. Cover and let sit for 5–6 min, then fluff with a fork.
2. In a skillet, heat olive oil and sauté chickpeas with harissa for 3–4 min until slightly crisped.
3. Add spinach to the pan and cook until wilted, 1–2 min.
4. Toss couscous with lemon juice and season lightly.
5. Assemble bowl with couscous, chickpeas, spinach, and crumbled feta.

▪ *Use rose harissa for a mild, aromatic heat.*

> *Nutritional Information (Per Serving):* **Calories: 490 kcal | Protein: 22g | Fat: 19g | Carbs: 28g | Fiber: 9g | Net Carbs: 19g**

FARRO SALAD WITH ROASTED EGGPLANT, TOMATOES & MINT YOGURT

🔔 1 serving   🟢 30 min   🟢 Oven, Stovetop

INGREDIENTS:

1/4 cup cooked farro (50g / ~1.8oz)
1/2 small eggplant, cubed (80g / ~2.8oz)
1/3 cup cherry tomatoes, halved (50g / ~1.8oz)
1/3 cup plain Greek yogurt (80g / ~2.8oz)
1 tbsp chopped walnuts (8g / ~0.28oz)

Also needed (not counted as main):
1 tbsp chopped fresh mint (3g / ~0.1oz)
1 tbsp olive oil (15ml / ~0.5oz)
Salt and pepper to taste

INSTRUCTIONS:

1. Preheat oven to 400°F (200°C). Toss eggplant with olive oil, salt, and pepper. Roast for 20 min, flipping once, until golden.
2. In a bowl, combine farro with roasted eggplant and cherry tomatoes.
3. Mix yogurt with chopped mint and season with salt and pepper.
4. Serve the farro salad warm or at room temperature with a dollop of mint yogurt and a sprinkle of walnuts.

▪ *Add a squeeze of lemon juice to the salad for brightness.*

> *Nutritional Information (Per Serving):* **Calories: 505 kcal | Protein: 21g | Fat: 21g | Carbs: 27g | Fiber: 8g | Net Carbs: 19g**

LENTIL AND BROWN RICE BOWL WITH LEMON TAHINI DRIZZLE

🔔 1 serving   ● 25 min   ● Stovetop

INGREDIENTS:

1/4 cup cooked brown rice (50g / ~1.8oz)
1/3 cup cooked green lentils (70g / ~2.5oz)
1 cup chopped baby spinach (30g / ~1oz)
1 tbsp tahini (15g / ~0.5oz)
1 tbsp lemon juice (15ml / ~0.5oz)

Also needed (not counted as main):
1/2 tbsp olive oil (7ml / ~0.25oz)
1/2 garlic clove, minced (2g / ~0.07oz)
Salt and pepper to taste

INSTRUCTIONS:

1. Heat olive oil in a skillet over medium. Add minced garlic and sauté 30 seconds, then add spinach and cook until wilted, 1–2 min.
2. In a bowl, combine cooked brown rice, lentils, and sautéed spinach. Season with a pinch of salt and pepper.
3. In a small bowl, whisk tahini, lemon juice, warm water, salt, and pepper until smooth and pourable.
4. Drizzle the sauce over the bowl just before serving. Serve warm with extra lemon on the side if desired.

■ *Use French lentils for a firmer texture.*

> *Nutritional Information (Per Serving):* **Calories: 495 kcal** | Protein: 22g | Fat: 18g | Carbs: 28g | Fiber: 9g | Net Carbs: 19g

QUINOA TABOULI WITH GRILLED CHICKEN, CUCUMBERS & POMEGRANATE

🔔 1 serving   ● 30 min   ● Stovetop, Grill

INGREDIENTS:

1/4 cup cooked quinoa (45g / ~1.6oz)
1/2 cup grilled chicken breast, sliced (75g / ~2.6oz)
1/4 cup diced cucumber (30g / ~1oz)
2 tbsp chopped parsley (8g / ~0.28oz)
1 tbsp pomegranate seeds (10g / ~0.35oz)

Also needed (not counted as main):
1 tbsp lemon juice (15ml / ~0.5oz)
1 tbsp olive oil (15ml / ~0.5oz)
Salt and black pepper to taste

INSTRUCTIONS:

1. In a large bowl, mix cooked quinoa with diced cucumber, parsley, lemon juice, olive oil, salt, and pepper. Stir well to combine.
2. Slice grilled chicken breast and arrange over the quinoa salad.
3. Sprinkle pomegranate seeds on top.
4. Serve immediately at room temperature or chilled. Optional: garnish with fresh mint or extra lemon juice.

■ *Add a few fresh mint leaves for a more classic tabouli flavor.*

> *Nutritional Information (Per Serving):* **Calories: 520 kcal** | Protein: 24g | Fat: 20g | Carbs: 26g | Fiber: 8g | Net Carbs: 18g

CHICKPEA & ROASTED CARROT BOWL WITH ZA'ATAR YOGURT

🔔 1 serving   ⏲ 25 min   🌿 Oven, Stovetop

INGREDIENTS:

1/3 cup canned chickpeas, rinsed and drained (60g / ~2.1oz)
1 medium carrot, sliced (80g / ~2.8oz)
1/3 cup plain Greek yogurt (80g / ~2.8oz)
1 tbsp olive oil (15ml / ~0.5oz)
1/4 tsp za'atar spice blend (1g / ~0.04oz)

Also needed (not counted as main):
1 tsp lemon juice (5ml / ~0.17oz)
Salt and pepper to taste

INSTRUCTIONS:

1. Preheat oven to 400°F (200°C). Toss sliced carrots and chickpeas with 1/2 tbsp olive oil, salt, and pepper.
2. Spread on a baking sheet and roast for 15–18 min until golden and tender.
3. In a small bowl, mix yogurt with lemon juice, za'atar, and a pinch of salt.
4. Assemble the bowl with roasted chickpeas and carrots, drizzle with remaining olive oil and za'atar yogurt.

■ *Add chopped parsley or toasted sesame seeds for texture.*

> *Nutritional Information (Per Serving):* **Calories: 490 kcal | Protein: 21g | Fat: 19g | Carbs: 28g | Fiber: 9g | Net Carbs: 19g**

BARLEY PILAF WITH ROASTED PEPPERS, OLIVES & HALLOUMI

🔔 1 serving   ⏲ 30 min   🌿 Stovetop

INGREDIENTS:

1/4 cup cooked pearl barley (55g / ~1.9oz)
1/4 cup diced roasted red pepper (40g / ~1.4oz)
1 oz halloumi cheese, cubed and seared (30g / ~1oz)
1 tbsp sliced Kalamata olives (10g / ~0.35oz)
1 tbsp olive oil (15ml / ~0.5oz)

Also needed (not counted as main):
1 tbsp chopped parsley (3g / ~0.1oz)
Salt and pepper to taste

INSTRUCTIONS:

1. Heat olive oil in a pan. Sear halloumi for 1–2 min per side until golden.
2. In a bowl, combine cooked barley, roasted pepper, olives, and parsley.
3. Toss with remaining oil, season with salt and pepper.
4. Top with warm halloumi and serve immediately.

■ *For extra zest, finish with a squeeze of lemon or a pinch of chili flakes.*

> *Nutritional Information (Per Serving):* **Calories: 525 kcal | Protein: 22g | Fat: 21g | Carbs: 27g | Fiber: 8g | Net Carbs: 19g**

BULGUR & GRILLED VEGETABLE BOWL WITH HERB PESTO

🔔 1 serving ● 25 min ● Stovetop, Grill

INGREDIENTS:

1/4 cup fine bulgur, dry (40g / ~1.4oz)
1/3 cup diced zucchini and bell pepper, grilled (70g / ~2.5oz)
1 tbsp grated Parmesan cheese (7g / ~0.25oz)
1 tbsp olive oil (15ml / ~0.5oz)
1 tbsp basil pesto (15g / ~0.5oz)

Also needed (not counted as main):
1 tbsp chopped parsley (3g / ~0.1oz)
Salt and black pepper to taste

INSTRUCTIONS:

1. Place bulgur in a heatproof bowl and pour over 1/3 cup (80ml) hot water. Cover and let steam for 10 min until tender, then fluff with a fork.
2. Meanwhile, preheat a grill pan or skillet over medium-high heat. Lightly brush zucchini and bell pepper slices with olive oil and grill for 4–5 min per side until charred and softened.
3. Chop the grilled vegetables into bite-size pieces and combine them with the cooked bulgur in a bowl.
4. Stir in Parmesan and parsley, drizzle with herb pesto and remaining olive oil. Season with salt and pepper to taste.

■ Use any leftover grilled vegetables or swap in eggplant or asparagus.

> *Nutritional Information (Per Serving):* **Calories: 510 kcal | Protein: 21g | Fat: 20g | Carbs: 28g | Fiber: 9g | Net Carbs: 19g**

MILLET SALAD WITH CHERRY TOMATOES, FETA & TOASTED PINE NUTS

🔔 1 serving ● 25 min ● Stovetop

INGREDIENTS:

1/4 cup cooked millet (50g / ~1.8oz)
1/3 cup cherry tomatoes, halved (50g / ~1.8oz)
2 tbsp crumbled feta cheese (30g / ~1oz)
1 tsp pine nuts, toasted (5g / ~0.18oz)
1 tbsp olive oil (15ml / ~0.5oz)

Also needed (not counted as main):
1 tbsp chopped mint or basil (3g / ~0.1oz)
1 tsp lemon juice (5ml / ~0.17oz)
Salt and pepper to taste

INSTRUCTIONS:

1. If not pre-cooked, cook millet in water until tender, then drain and let cool slightly.
2. Toast pine nuts in a dry skillet for 2–3 min until golden.
3. In a bowl, mix warm millet with olive oil, lemon juice, salt, and pepper.
4. Add cherry tomatoes, feta, and herbs. Toss gently to combine.
5. Top with toasted pine nuts and serve at room temperature.

■ For extra protein, add a few chickpeas or grilled tofu cubes.

> *Nutritional Information (Per Serving):* **Calories: 495 kcal | Protein: 22g | Fat: 19g | Carbs: 25g | Fiber: 8g | Net Carbs: 17g**

CHAPTER 7: Light Mediterranean Mains

SEARED TUNA WITH WHITE BEANS, DILL & TOMATO RELISH

🔔 1 serving   🟢 20 min   🌿 Stovetop

INGREDIENTS:

4 oz tuna steak (115g / ~4oz)
1/3 cup canned white beans, rinsed (70g / ~2.5oz)
1/4 cup cherry tomatoes, chopped (40g / ~1.4oz)
1 tbsp chopped fresh dill (3g / ~0.1oz)
1 tbsp olive oil (15ml / ~0.5oz)

Also needed (not counted as main):
1 tsp lemon juice (5ml / ~0.17oz)
Salt and pepper to taste

INSTRUCTIONS:

1. Season tuna with salt and pepper. Heat 1/2 tbsp olive oil in a skillet and sear tuna 2–3 min per side until just pink in center.
2. In a bowl, mix white beans with dill, lemon juice, 1/2 tbsp olive oil, and a pinch of salt.
3. Combine chopped cherry tomatoes with a pinch of salt and pepper to make a quick relish.
4. Plate tuna over the bean mixture, top with tomato relish, and serve warm.

▪ *For extra zest, add lemon zest or a few capers to the tomato relish.*

> *Nutritional Information (Per Serving):* **Calories: 520 kcal | Protein: 24g | Fat: 21g | Carbs: 26g | Fiber: 9g | Net Carbs: 17g**

GRILLED CHICKEN WITH ARTICHOKES, CUCUMBER & OLIVE SALSA

🔔 1 serving   🟢 25 min   🌿 Grill, Stovetop

INGREDIENTS:

4 oz chicken breast, boneless (115g / ~4oz)
1/4 cup canned artichoke hearts, chopped (40g / ~1.4oz)
1/4 cup diced cucumber (30g / ~1oz)
1 tbsp chopped Kalamata olives (10g / ~0.35oz)
1 tbsp olive oil (15ml / ~0.5oz)

Also needed (not counted as main):
1 tbsp chopped parsley (3g / ~0.1oz)
1 tsp red wine vinegar (5ml / ~0.17oz)
Salt and black pepper to taste

INSTRUCTIONS:

1. Season chicken with salt and pepper. Grill or sear over medium heat for 5–6 min per side until cooked through. Let rest.
2. In a bowl, mix artichokes, cucumber, olives, parsley, olive oil, and vinegar.
3. Slice chicken and serve topped with the olive salsa.

▪ *Add a pinch of oregano or sumac to the salsa for a deeper Mediterranean flavor.*

> *Nutritional Information (Per Serving):* **Calories: 505 kcal | Protein: 23g | Fat: 20g | Carbs: 18g | Fiber: 8g | Net Carbs: 10g**

BAKED COD WITH HERBED COUSCOUS AND LEMON-TOMATO SAUCE

🔔 1 serving   ⏱ 25 min   🌿 Oven, Stovetop

INGREDIENTS:

4 oz cod fillet (115g / ~4oz)
1/4 cup dry couscous (40g / ~1.4oz)
1/4 cup crushed tomatoes (60g / ~2.1oz)
1 tbsp chopped fresh parsley (3g / ~0.1oz)
1 tbsp olive oil (15ml / ~0.5oz)

Also needed (not counted as main):
1 tsp lemon juice (5ml / ~0.17oz)
Salt, pepper, and a pinch of dried oregano

INSTRUCTIONS:

1. Preheat oven to 375°F (190°C). Season cod with salt, pepper, and oregano. Bake for 12–15 min until flaky.
2. Meanwhile, pour 1/3 cup hot water over couscous. Cover and let sit 5 min, then fluff with a fork and stir in parsley and 1/2 tbsp olive oil.
3. In a small pan, warm tomatoes with lemon juice and a pinch of salt. Simmer for 3–4 min.
4. Plate couscous, top with cod, and spoon tomato sauce over the fish. Drizzle with remaining olive oil.

■ Add a bit of lemon zest to couscous for extra aroma.

Nutritional Information (Per Serving): **Calories: 495 kcal | Protein: 24g | Fat: 19g | Carbs: 26g | Fiber: 9g | Net Carbs: 17g**

TURKEY PATTIES WITH QUINOA TABBOULEH & YOGURT DIP

🔔 1 serving   ⏱ 30 min   🌿 Stovetop

INGREDIENTS:

4 oz ground turkey (115g / ~4oz)
1/4 cup cooked quinoa (45g / ~1.6oz)
2 tbsp diced cucumber (20g / ~0.7oz)
2 tbsp plain Greek yogurt (30g / ~1oz)
1 tbsp chopped parsley (3g / ~0.1oz)

Also needed (not counted as main):
1 tsp lemon juice (5ml / ~0.17oz)
1/4 tsp ground cumin (0.5g / ~0.02oz)
Salt and pepper to taste

INSTRUCTIONS:

1. Mix turkey with cumin, salt, and pepper. Form into 2 small patties.
2. Heat a skillet with 1/2 tbsp olive oil and cook patties 4–5 min per side until golden and cooked through.
3. In a bowl, combine quinoa, cucumber, parsley, lemon juice, and 1/2 tbsp olive oil. Season lightly.
4. Stir yogurt with a pinch of salt and serve as a dip.
5. Plate patties alongside quinoa tabbouleh with yogurt on the side.

■ Add mint or scallions to the tabbouleh for extra brightness.

Nutritional Information (Per Serving): **Calories: 530 kcal | Protein: 25g | Fat: 20g | Carbs: 24g | Fiber: 8g | Net Carbs: 16g**

SHRIMP SKEWERS WITH BULGUR, ZUCCHINI & PARSLEY VINAIGRETTE

🔔 1 serving   ● 25 min   ● Grill, Stovetop

INGREDIENTS:

4 oz raw shrimp, peeled and deveined (115g / ~4oz)
1/4 cup dry bulgur (40g / ~1.4oz)
1/2 small zucchini, sliced (60g / ~2.1oz)
1 tbsp chopped fresh parsley (3g / ~0.1oz)
1 tbsp olive oil (15ml / ~0.5oz)

Also needed (not counted as main):
1 tsp lemon juice (5ml / ~0.17oz)
Salt and black pepper to taste

INSTRUCTIONS:

1. Soak bulgur in 1/3 cup hot water, cover, and let sit 10 min. Fluff with fork.
2. Toss shrimp with salt, pepper, and 1/2 tbsp olive oil. Thread onto skewers with zucchini.
3. Grill skewers for 2–3 min per side until shrimp are opaque and zucchini is tender.
4. Whisk parsley, lemon juice, and remaining olive oil into a vinaigrette.
5. Serve shrimp and zucchini over bulgur, drizzled with vinaigrette.

■ *Add a pinch of cumin or paprika to the shrimp for extra depth.*

> *Nutritional Information (Per Serving):* **Calories: 510 kcal | Protein: 24g | Fat: 20g | Carbs: 26g | Fiber: 8g | Net Carbs: 18g**

SARDINE SALAD WITH FENNEL, ORANGE & TOASTED ALMONDS

🔔 1 serving   ● 20 min   ● No-Cook

INGREDIENTS:

1 can sardines in olive oil, drained (3.5 oz / 100g)
1/2 cup shaved fennel (50g / ~1.8oz)
1/2 small orange, segmented (60g / ~2.1oz)
1 tbsp sliced almonds, toasted (8g / ~0.28oz)
1 tbsp olive oil (15ml / ~0.5oz)

Also needed (not counted as main):
1 tsp lemon juice (5ml / ~0.17oz)
Salt and black pepper to taste

INSTRUCTIONS:

1. In a medium bowl, mix shaved fennel and orange segments. Let sit 2–3 min to lightly marinate.
2. Add drained sardines, then drizzle with olive oil and lemon juice. Season with salt and black pepper to taste.
3. Gently fold the ingredients together with a spoon, keeping the sardines mostly whole.
4. Sprinkle toasted almonds on top just before serving.

■ *Use blood orange or grapefruit for a twist.*

> *Nutritional Information (Per Serving):* **Calories: 495 kcal | Protein: 22g | Fat: 23g | Carbs: 16g | Fiber: 9g | Net Carbs: 7g**

ROASTED SALMON WITH LENTILS, SPINACH & MUSTARD DRESSING

🔔 1 serving ● 25 min ● Oven + Stovetop

INGREDIENTS:

4 oz salmon fillet (115g / ~4oz)
1/2 cup cooked green lentils (100g / ~3.5oz)
1 cup baby spinach (30g / ~1oz)
1 tbsp olive oil (15ml / ~0.5oz)
1 tsp whole grain mustard (5g / ~0.17oz)

Also needed (not counted as main):
1 tsp lemon juice (5ml / ~0.17oz)
Salt and black pepper to taste

INSTRUCTIONS:

1. Preheat oven to 400°F (200°C). Season salmon with salt and pepper and roast skin-side down for 12–14 min until just cooked through.
2. Meanwhile, warm lentils in a small pan with 1 tsp olive oil. Stir in spinach and cook for 1–2 min until just wilted.
3. In a bowl, whisk remaining olive oil with mustard and lemon juice.
4. Serve salmon over lentils and spinach. Drizzle with dressing before serving.

■ *Try with arugula or baby kale for a peppery green swap.*

Nutritional Information (Per Serving): **Calories: 510 kcal | Protein: 25g | Fat: 21g | Carbs: 22g | Fiber: 9g | Net Carbs: 13g**

GRILLED EGGPLANT STACK WITH RICOTTA, TOMATOES & BASIL OIL

🔔 1 serving ● 25 min ● Grill

INGREDIENTS:

4 slices eggplant, 1/2-inch thick (120g / ~4.2oz)
1/2 cup ricotta cheese (125g / ~4.4oz)
1 medium tomato, sliced (80g / ~2.8oz)
1 tbsp olive oil (15ml / ~0.5oz)
1 tbsp chopped fresh basil (3g / ~0.1oz)

Also needed (not counted as main):
Salt and pepper to taste
Optional: 1/4 tsp balsamic vinegar (1ml / ~0.03oz)

INSTRUCTIONS:

1. Preheat grill or grill pan over medium heat. Brush eggplant slices with olive oil on both sides. Grill for 3–4 min per side until tender and charred.
2. In a bowl, mix ricotta with chopped basil, salt, and pepper.
3. Stack grilled eggplant slices with a layer of tomato and a spoonful of basil ricotta between each.
4. Drizzle with a bit of olive oil and a splash of balsamic if using. Serve warm or at room temperature.

■ *For more tang, add a few capers or olives between the layers.*

Nutritional Information (Per Serving): **Calories: 495 kcal | Protein: 22g | Fat: 20g | Carbs: 19g | Fiber: 8g | Net Carbs: 11g**

CHAPTER 8: Nourishing One-Pan & Sheet-Pan Meals

ONE-PAN CHICKEN WITH ZUCCHINI, RED ONION & OLIVES

🔔 1 serving   🟢 25 min   🌿 Stovetop

INGREDIENTS:

4 oz chicken breast, cubed (115g / ~4oz)
1/2 medium zucchini, sliced (75g / ~2.6oz)
1/4 small red onion, sliced (40g / ~1.4oz)
6 Kalamata olives, halved (30g / ~1oz)
1 tbsp olive oil (15ml / ~0.5oz)

Also needed (not counted as main):
1/2 tsp dried oregano (1g / ~0.036oz)
1 garlic clove, minced (3g / ~0.1oz)
Salt and black pepper to taste

INSTRUCTIONS:

1. Heat olive oil in a skillet over medium heat. Add chicken, season with salt and pepper, and cook for 5–6 min until browned.
2. Add garlic, zucchini, and red onion. Sauté for 6–8 min until tender.
3. Stir in olives and oregano. Cook 2 more min to blend flavors.
4. Serve warm straight from the pan.

▪ Add a squeeze of lemon juice before serving for extra brightness.

> **Nutritional Information (Per Serving):** Calories: 520 kcal | Protein: 25g | Fat: 21g | Carbs: 18g | Fiber: 9g | Net Carbs: 9g

SHEET-PAN SHRIMP WITH SWEET POTATO, FETA & LEMON OIL

🔔 1 serving   🟢 25 min   🌿 Oven

INGREDIENTS:

4 oz raw shrimp, peeled and deveined (115g / ~4oz)
1/2 medium sweet potato, diced (100g / ~3.5oz)
2 tbsp crumbled feta (30g / ~1oz)
1 tbsp olive oil (15ml / ~0.5oz)
1 tsp lemon zest (2g / ~0.07oz)

Also needed (not counted as main):
1/4 tsp ground cumin (0.5g / ~0.018oz)
Salt and black pepper to taste

INSTRUCTIONS:

1. Preheat oven to 400°F (200°C). Line a sheet pan with parchment.
2. Toss sweet potato with half the olive oil, cumin, salt, and pepper. Roast for 15 min.
3. Add shrimp to the pan, drizzle with remaining oil and lemon zest. Roast 7–8 min until shrimp are pink and sweet potato tender.
4. Top with feta and serve warm.

▪ Add fresh parsley or arugula on top for freshness.

> **Nutritional Information (Per Serving):** Calories: 545 kcal | Protein: 24g | Fat: 22g | Carbs: 26g | Fiber: 8g | Net Carbs: 18g

TURKEY & VEGETABLE RAGÙ WITH TOMATOES, GARLIC & OREGANO

🔔 1 serving ● 25 min ● Stovetop

INGREDIENTS:

4 oz ground turkey (115g / ~4oz)
1/3 cup chopped zucchini (60g / ~2.1oz)
1/3 cup chopped red bell pepper (50g / ~1.8oz)
1/2 cup crushed canned tomatoes (120g / ~4.2oz)
1 tbsp olive oil (15ml / ~0.5oz)

Also needed (not counted as main):
1 garlic clove, minced (3g / ~0.1oz)
1/2 tsp dried oregano (1g / ~0.036oz)
Salt and pepper to taste

INSTRUCTIONS:

1. Heat olive oil in a skillet over medium heat. Add garlic and cook 30 sec.
2. Add ground turkey and cook for 5–6 min, breaking into crumbles.
3. Stir in zucchini and bell pepper, cook for 4–5 min until softened.
4. Pour in tomatoes, add oregano, and simmer uncovered for 8–10 min until thickened.
5. Season with salt and pepper, then serve warm.

■ *Add a few capers or olives for deeper flavor.*

> *Nutritional Information (Per Serving):* **Calories: 510 kcal | Protein: 24g | Fat: 20g | Carbs: 22g | Fiber: 8g | Net Carbs: 13g**

SKILLET LAMB WITH SPINACH, CHICKPEAS & CUMIN

🔔 1 serving ● 25 min ● Stovetop

INGREDIENTS:

4 oz ground lamb (115g / ~4oz)
1 cup baby spinach (30g / ~1oz)
1/3 cup cooked chickpeas, drained (60g / ~2.1oz)
1/4 cup diced red onion (40g / ~1.4oz)
1 tbsp olive oil (15ml / ~0.5oz)

Also needed (not counted as main):
1/2 tsp ground cumin (1g / ~0.036oz)
Salt and pepper to taste

INSTRUCTIONS:

1. Heat olive oil in a skillet over medium heat. Add red onion and cook 2 min.
2. Add lamb, season with cumin, salt, and pepper. Cook for 6–7 min until browned.
3. Stir in chickpeas and cook 2–3 min to heat through.
4. Add spinach and cook 1–2 min until wilted.

■ *Top with a spoon of Greek yogurt or chopped parsley if desired.*

> *Nutritional Information (Per Serving):* **Calories: 540 kcal | Protein: 23g | Fat: 22g | Carbs: 24g | Fiber: 8g | Net Carbs: 16g**

BAKED HALIBUT WITH PEPPERS, POTATOES & ROSEMARY

🔔 1 serving   ⏲ 25 min   🔥 Oven

INGREDIENTS:

5 oz halibut fillet, skinless (140g / ~5oz)
1/2 cup red bell pepper, chopped (60g / ~2.1oz)
1/2 small waxy potato, thinly sliced (70g / ~2.5oz)
1 tbsp olive oil (15ml / ~0.5oz)
1 tsp fresh rosemary, chopped (1g / ~0.036oz)

Also needed (not counted as main):
1 small garlic clove, minced (3g / ~0.1oz)
Salt and pepper to taste
Lemon wedge to serve

INSTRUCTIONS:

1. Preheat oven to 400°F (200°C).
2. Toss potatoes and peppers with 1/2 tbsp olive oil, garlic, rosemary, salt, and pepper. Spread on a parchment-lined baking tray.
3. Roast for 10–12 min, then add halibut on top. Drizzle with remaining oil and season.
4. Bake another 10–12 min, until the fish is opaque and flakes easily.
5. Serve with a squeeze of lemon.

▪ *Add capers or olives for a salty twist.*

> *Nutritional Information (Per Serving):* **Calories: 540 kcal | Protein: 24g | Fat: 22g | Carbs: 26g | Fiber: 8g | Net Carbs: 18g**

EGGPLANT AND LENTIL BAKE WITH GARLIC YOGURT & PARSLEY

🔔 1 serving   ⏲ 30 min   🔥 Oven

INGREDIENTS:

1/2 medium eggplant, cubed (100g / ~3.5oz)
1/2 cup cooked green lentils (90g / ~3.2oz)
2 tbsp plain Greek yogurt (30g / ~1oz)
1 tbsp olive oil (15ml / ~0.5oz)
1 tbsp fresh parsley, chopped (3g / ~0.1oz)

Also needed (not counted as main):
1 small garlic clove, minced (3g / ~0.1oz)
Salt and pepper to taste
1 tbsp lemon juice (15ml / ~0.5oz)

INSTRUCTIONS:

1. Preheat oven to 400°F (200°C).
2. Toss eggplant with olive oil, salt, and pepper. Roast for 15–20 min until golden.
3. Meanwhile, mash garlic into yogurt with lemon juice and a pinch of salt.
4. Combine roasted eggplant and warm lentils in a bowl. Spoon over garlic yogurt and sprinkle with parsley.

▪ *Add a pinch of cumin or sumac for extra depth.*

> *Nutritional Information (Per Serving):* **Calories: 510 kcal | Protein: 21g | Fat: 20g | Carbs: 28g | Fiber: 9g | Net Carbs: 19g**

MEDITERRANEAN MEATBALL TRAY WITH TOMATOES & CHICKPEAS

🔔 1 serving ● 30 min ● Oven

INGREDIENTS:

4 oz ground beef or lamb (115g / ~4oz)
1/2 cup canned chickpeas, rinsed (90g / ~3.2oz)
1/2 cup cherry tomatoes, whole or halved (75g / ~2.6oz)
1 tbsp olive oil (15ml / ~0.5oz)
1 tbsp fresh parsley, chopped (3g / ~0.1oz)

Also needed (not counted as main):
1/2 tsp ground cumin (1g / ~0.036oz)
1 garlic clove, finely minced (3g / ~0.1oz)
Salt and black pepper to taste

INSTRUCTIONS:

1. Preheat oven to 400°F (200°C).
2. In a bowl, mix ground meat with cumin, garlic, salt, and pepper. Form into small meatballs.
3. On a parchment-lined tray, arrange meatballs, chickpeas, and cherry tomatoes. Drizzle with olive oil.
4. Roast for 20–22 minutes, shaking the tray once halfway through.
5. Sprinkle with chopped parsley and serve warm.

■ *Add a dollop of yogurt or drizzle with tahini before serving.*

> *Nutritional Information (Per Serving):* **Calories: 520 kcal | Protein: 24g | Fat: 22g | Carbs: 26g | Fiber: 9g | Net Carbs: 17g**

CHICKPEA SHAKSHUKA WITH SPINACH, HARISSA & POACHED EGG

🔔 1 serving ● 25 min ● Stovetop

INGREDIENTS:

1/2 cup canned chickpeas, rinsed (90g / ~3.2oz)
1/2 cup canned diced tomatoes (120g / ~4.2oz)
1 cup spinach leaves, fresh (30g / ~1oz)
1 large egg (50g / ~1.8oz)
1 tbsp olive oil (15ml / ~0.5oz)

Also needed (not counted as main):
1 tsp harissa paste (5g / ~0.17oz)
1 garlic clove, finely chopped (3g / ~0.1oz)
Salt and pepper to taste

INSTRUCTIONS:

1. Heat olive oil in a skillet over medium heat. Sauté garlic and harissa for 30 seconds.
2. Add chickpeas, tomatoes, and a pinch of salt.
3. Simmer for 5–7 minutes until slightly thickened.
4. Stir in spinach and cook until wilted.
5. Make a small well and crack in the egg. Cover and cook 5–6 minutes until the egg white is set.
6. Serve warm with herbs or a spoonful of yogurt, if desired.

■ *Use smoked paprika for a deeper flavor.*

> *Nutritional Information (Per Serving):* **Calories: 495 kcal | Protein: 22g | Fat: 21g | Carbs: 29g | Fiber: 10g | Net Carbs: 19g**

CHAPTER 9: Fresh Salads & Cold Lunches

ORZO SALAD WITH TUNA, CHERRY TOMATOES & BASIL VINAIGRETTE

🔔 1 serving   🟢 20 min   🍃 No-Cook

INGREDIENTS:

1/3 cup cooked orzo (55g / ~1.9oz)
3 oz canned tuna in olive oil, drained (85g / ~3oz)
1/2 cup cherry tomatoes, halved (75g / ~2.6oz)
1 cup baby arugula or spinach (30g / ~1oz)
1 tbsp olive oil (15ml / ~0.5oz)

Also needed (not counted as main):
1 tbsp chopped fresh basil (3g / ~0.1oz)
1 tsp white wine vinegar (5ml / ~0.17oz)
Salt and pepper to taste

INSTRUCTIONS:

1. In a small bowl, whisk together the olive oil, white wine vinegar, chopped basil, salt, and pepper until well emulsified. Set aside.
2. In a larger mixing bowl, add the cooked orzo, drained tuna (flaked with a fork), halved cherry tomatoes, and fresh baby arugula or spinach.
3. Pour the basil vinaigrette over the salad and toss gently until everything is evenly coated without breaking the tuna pieces too much.
4. Serve immediately or chill briefly. Garnish with basil if desired.

■ *Add a few capers for briny contrast.*

> **Nutritional Information (Per Serving):** Calories: 545 kcal | Protein: 24g | Fat: 22g | Carbs: 28g | Fiber: 8g | Net Carbs: 20g

ROASTED BEET SALAD WITH CHICKPEAS, DILL & LEMON YOGURT

🔔 1 serving   🟢 20 min   🍃 Oven

INGREDIENTS:

1/2 cup roasted beets, diced (80g / ~2.8oz)
1/3 cup canned chickpeas, rinsed (60g / ~2.1oz)
1/4 cup plain Greek yogurt, 2% (60g / ~2.1oz)
1 tbsp olive oil (15ml / ~0.5oz)
1 tbsp chopped fresh dill (3g / ~0.1oz)

Also needed (not counted as main):
1 tsp lemon juice (5ml / ~0.17oz)
Salt and pepper to taste

INSTRUCTIONS:

1. If beets aren't pre-roasted, wrap diced raw beets in foil and roast at 400°F (200°C) for 20 minutes or until tender. Let cool slightly.
2. In a bowl, mix the Greek yogurt with lemon juice, chopped dill, salt, and pepper until smooth. Chill until ready to use.
3. In another bowl, combine roasted beets and rinsed chickpeas. Drizzle with olive oil and toss to coat evenly.
4. Top with dill yogurt and serve in a bowl or on a plate.
5. Serve at room temperature or slightly chilled for a refreshing balance.

■ *Add a sprinkle of toasted walnuts for crunch.*

> **Nutritional Information (Per Serving):** Calories: 510 kcal | Protein: 21g | Fat: 21g | Carbs: 27g | Fiber: 9g | Net Carbs: 18g

HALLOUMI & WATERMELON SALAD WITH CUCUMBER & MINT

🔔 1 serving ● 15 min ● Stovetop

INGREDIENTS:

3 oz halloumi cheese, sliced (85g / ~3 oz)
3/4 cup watermelon, cubed (115g / ~4 oz)
1/2 cup cucumber, sliced (75g / ~2.6 oz)
1 tbsp fresh mint, chopped (2g / ~0.07 oz)
1 tbsp olive oil (15ml / ~0.5 oz)

Also needed (not counted as main):
1 tsp lemon juice (5ml / ~0.17 oz)
Black pepper to taste

INSTRUCTIONS:

1. Heat a nonstick skillet over medium heat. Add the halloumi slices and sear for 1–2 minutes per side until golden and lightly crisp. Remove from heat.
2. In a mixing bowl, combine the watermelon cubes, cucumber slices, and chopped mint.
3. Drizzle with olive oil and lemon juice, and gently toss to coat the ingredients evenly.
4. Transfer the salad to a plate or bowl, top with the warm grilled halloumi, and season with freshly ground black pepper.

■ *For extra freshness, chill the watermelon cubes before serving.*

> *Nutritional Information (Per Serving):* **Calories: 510 kcal | Protein: 22g | Fat: 23g | Carbs: 22g | Fiber: 8g | Net Carbs: 14g**

WHITE BEAN SALAD WITH SARDINES, ARUGULA & CAPERS

🔔 1 serving ● 10 min ● No-Cook

INGREDIENTS:

1/2 cup canned white beans, rinsed (130g / ~4.6 oz)
1 can sardines in olive oil, drained (3.5 oz / 100g)
1 cup arugula (30g / ~1 oz)
1 tsp capers, rinsed (5g / ~0.18 oz)
1 tbsp olive oil (15ml / ~0.5 oz)

Also needed (not counted as main):
1 tsp red wine vinegar (5ml / ~0.17 oz)
Salt and black pepper to taste

INSTRUCTIONS:

1. Rinse and drain the canned white beans thoroughly.
2. In a bowl, combine the beans with arugula, drained sardines, and rinsed capers.
3. Drizzle with olive oil and red wine vinegar, then season lightly with salt and black pepper.
4. Toss gently to avoid breaking up the sardines too much. Serve chilled or at room temperature.

■ *Add a few thin red onion slices for a sharper kick.*

> *Nutritional Information (Per Serving):* **Calories: 490 kcal | Protein: 23g | Fat: 21g | Carbs: 24g | Fiber: 9g | Net Carbs: 15g**

GRILLED CHICKEN SALAD WITH QUINOA, FIGS & WALNUTS

🔔 1 serving ● 25 min ● Stovetop

INGREDIENTS:

4 oz grilled chicken breast, sliced (115g)
1/4 cup cooked quinoa (43g / ~1.5oz)
1/4 cup chopped fresh figs (40g / ~1.4oz)
1 tbsp chopped walnuts (7g / ~0.25oz)
1 cup mixed greens (30g / ~1oz)
1 tbsp olive oil (15ml / ~0.5oz)

Also needed:
1 tsp balsamic vinegar (5ml / ~0.17oz),
Salt and black pepper to taste

INSTRUCTIONS:

1. Grill the chicken breast on a stovetop grill pan or skillet over medium heat for 5–6 minutes per side, until fully cooked. Let it rest for 2 minutes, then slice.
2. In a medium bowl, combine the mixed greens, cooked quinoa, chopped figs, and chopped walnuts.
3. Top the salad with the warm sliced chicken.
4. Drizzle with olive oil and balsamic vinegar. Season with salt and pepper to taste.
5. Toss gently to coat and serve immediately or chill briefly for a cooler salad.

▪ *Swap figs for grapes if out of season.*

> *Nutritional Information (Per Serving):* **Calories: 540 kcal | Protein: 24g | Fat: 22g | Carbs: 28g | Fiber: 9g | Net Carbs: 19g**

COUSCOUS SALAD WITH ROASTED VEGETABLES & ZA'ATAR DRESSING

🔔 1 serving ● 25 min ● Oven, No-Cook

INGREDIENTS:

1/4 cup cooked couscous (43g / ~1.5oz)
1/4 cup roasted bell peppers & zucchini, chopped (50g / ~1.8oz)
1 tbsp crumbled feta cheese (15g / ~0.5oz)
1 tbsp olive oil (15ml / ~0.5oz)
1 cup arugula or spinach (30g / ~1oz)

Also needed:
1/2 tsp za'atar spice mix (1g / ~0.036oz),
1 tsp lemon juice (5ml / ~0.17oz),
Salt and black pepper to taste

INSTRUCTIONS:

1. If needed, cook the couscous per package instructions and let it cool.
2. Preheat oven to 400°F (200°C). Roast chopped bell peppers and zucchini with olive oil for 15–18 min until tender and golden.
3. Whisk olive oil, lemon juice, za'atar, salt, and pepper in a bowl.
4. Add couscous and toss with dressing. Stir in roasted vegetables, arugula or spinach, and feta.
5. Serve at room temperature or slightly chilled.

▪ *Add a few pomegranate seeds for a sweet contrast.*

> *Nutritional Information (Per Serving):* **Calories: 505 kcal | Protein: 21g | Fat: 20g | Carbs: 29g | Fiber: 8g | Net Carbs: 21g**

LENTIL & TOMATO SALAD WITH FETA, OLIVES & FRESH THYME

🛎 1 serving ● 25 min ● No-Cook

INGREDIENTS:

1/2 cup cooked green lentils (100g / ~3.5oz)
1/2 cup cherry tomatoes, halved (75g / ~2.6oz)
2 tbsp crumbled feta cheese (30g / ~1oz)
1 tbsp pitted black olives, sliced (15g / ~0.5oz)
1 tbsp extra virgin olive oil (15ml / ~0.5oz)

Also needed (not counted as main):
1 tsp red wine vinegar (5ml / ~0.17oz)
1/2 tsp fresh thyme leaves (1g / ~0.04oz)
Salt and black pepper to taste

INSTRUCTIONS:

1. Place the cooked lentils in a medium bowl. Drizzle with olive oil and red wine vinegar, then season with salt, pepper, and fresh thyme leaves. Toss gently to coat.
2. Add the halved cherry tomatoes and sliced olives. Fold in the crumbled feta last to keep some texture.
3. Let the salad sit at room temperature for 5–10 minutes to allow the flavors to combine.
4. Serve chilled or at room temperature for a refreshing, protein-rich lunch.

■ *For added crunch, top with chopped cucumber or pumpkin seeds.*

> *Nutritional Information (Per Serving):* **Calories: 485 kcal | Protein: 21g | Fat: 22g | Carbs: 28g | Fiber: 9g | Net Carbs: 19g**

SUMMER BULGUR SALAD WITH SHRIMP, AVOCADO & CITRUS OIL

🛎 1 serving ● 25 min ● Stovetop

INGREDIENTS:

1/2 cup cooked bulgur (85g / ~3oz)
4 oz cooked shrimp, peeled (115g / ~4oz)
1/4 ripe avocado, diced (50g / ~1.8oz)
1 tbsp lemon juice (15ml / ~0.5oz)
1 tbsp olive oil (15ml / ~0.5oz)

Also needed (not counted as main):
1 tsp orange zest (2g / ~0.07oz)
1 tbsp chopped parsley (4g / ~0.14oz)
Salt and black pepper to taste

INSTRUCTIONS:

1. If using raw shrimp, cook them in a skillet over medium heat for 2–3 minutes per side until pink and opaque. Let cool.
2. In a small bowl, whisk together the olive oil, lemon juice, orange zest, salt, and black pepper.
3. In a large bowl, combine cooked and cooled bulgur, shrimp, diced avocado, and chopped parsley.
4. Pour the citrus dressing over the mixture and toss gently to combine.
5. Serve immediately or chill for 10 minutes for a cooling lunch option.

■ *Swap parsley for fresh mint for a brighter twist.*

> *Nutritional Information (Per Serving):* **Calories: 535 kcal | Protein: 24g | Fat: 23g | Carbs: 29g | Fiber: 8g | Net Carbs: 21g**

SNACK: CHAPTER 10: Baked Mediterranean Treats

BAKED FIGS WITH WALNUTS, HONEY & ORANGE ZEST

🔔 1 serving   ● 15 min   ● Oven

INGREDIENTS:

2 fresh figs, halved (80g / ~2.8oz)
1 tbsp chopped walnuts (8g / ~0.28oz)
1 tsp honey (7g / ~0.25oz)
1/4 tsp grated orange zest (1g / ~0.04oz)
1/2 tsp olive oil (2.5ml / ~0.08oz)

Also needed (not counted as main):
Pinch of cinnamon, optional

INSTRUCTIONS:

1. Preheat oven to 375°F (190°C).
2. Place halved figs cut-side up in a small baking dish.
3. Drizzle with olive oil and honey, then sprinkle with walnuts, orange zest, and a pinch of cinnamon if desired.
4. Bake for 10–12 minutes until soft and caramelized.
5. Let cool slightly before serving warm or at room temperature.

▪ *Try serving over a spoonful of Greek yogurt for extra protein.*

> **Nutritional Information (Per Serving):** Calories: 190 kcal | Protein: 8g | Fat: 9g | Carbs: 24g | Fiber: 5g | Net Carbs: 19g

SPICED APPLE & DATE CRUMBLE WITH OLIVE OIL STREUSEL

🔔 1 serving   ● 25 min   ● Oven

INGREDIENTS:

1/2 small apple, diced (60g / ~2.1oz)
1 Medjool date, chopped (20g / ~0.7oz)
1 tbsp rolled oats (8g / ~0.28oz)
1 tsp almond flour (3g / ~0.1oz)
1/2 tbsp olive oil (7ml / ~0.25oz)

Also needed (not counted as main):
1/4 tsp cinnamon
Pinch of salt
2 tsp water (10ml / ~0.34oz)

INSTRUCTIONS:

1. Preheat oven to 375°F (190°C).
2. In a ramekin, mix diced apple, chopped date, cinnamon, water, and a pinch of salt.
3. In a small bowl, mix oats, almond flour, and olive oil until crumbly.
4. Sprinkle crumble mixture over the fruit.
5. Bake for 15 minutes until fruit is soft and topping is golden. Let cool slightly before serving.

▪ *Add plain yogurt on top for a creamy contrast.*

> **Nutritional Information (Per Serving):** Calories: 210 kcal | Protein: 9g | Fat: 8g | Carbs: 27g | Fiber: 4g | Net Carbs: 23g

ALMOND & RICOTTA CAKE WITH LEMON SYRUP GLAZE

🛎 1 serving ● 25 min ● Oven

INGREDIENTS:

2 tbsp almond flour (14g / ~0.5oz)
2 tbsp part-skim ricotta cheese (30g / ~1oz)
1 tsp low carb sweetener (4g / ~0.14oz)
1/4 tsp lemon zest (1g / ~0.04oz)
1/2 tsp lemon juice (2.5ml / ~0.08oz)
1/2 tsp olive oil (2.5ml / ~0.08oz)
1/4 tsp baking powder (1g / ~0.04oz)
1 small egg (50g / ~1.8oz)

Also needed (not counted as main):
Pinch of sea salt

INSTRUCTIONS:

1. Preheat oven to 350°F (175°C). Grease a small ramekin or muffin cup.
2. In a bowl, mix ricotta, egg, lemon zest, juice, olive oil, and sweetener.
3. Add almond flour, baking powder, and salt. Stir to form a smooth batter.
4. Pour into prepared ramekin and bake for 18–20 minutes, or until golden and set.
5. Let cool, then drizzle with a drop of lemon juice mixed with a pinch of sweetener.

■ *Serve with a few crushed toasted almonds on top for texture.*

Nutritional Information (Per Serving): **Calories: 210 kcal | Protein: 9g | Fat: 9g | Carbs: 10g | Fiber: 4g | Net Carbs: 4g**

PISTACHIO & APRICOT BISCOTTI WITH ORANGE BLOSSOM

🛎 1 serving ● 25 min ● Oven

INGREDIENTS:

1 tbsp chopped pistachios (10g / ~0.35oz)
1 tbsp chopped dried apricots (10g / ~0.35oz)
2 tbsp almond flour (14g / ~0.5oz)
1 tbsp oat fiber or coconut flour (7g / ~0.25oz)
1 tsp low carb sweetener (4g / ~0.14oz)
1/4 tsp orange blossom water (1.25ml / ~0.04oz)
1/2 tsp olive oil (2.5ml / ~0.08oz)
1 small egg white (30g / ~1oz)

Also needed (not counted as main):
1/4 tsp baking powder
Pinch of salt

INSTRUCTIONS:

1. Preheat oven to 350°F (175°C) and line a small baking tray.
2. In a bowl, whisk egg white until frothy. Mix in sweetener, orange blossom water, and olive oil.
3. Stir in almond flour, oat fiber, baking powder, pistachios, and apricots until a sticky dough forms.
4. Shape into a small log and bake for 15 minutes. Cool, slice, and rebake 5 minutes per side until crisp.

■ *Let them cool fully to achieve the perfect biscotti crunch.*

Nutritional Information (Per Serving): **Calories: 220 kcal | Protein: 8g | Fat: 8g | Carbs: 18g | Fiber: 5g | Net Carbs: 13g**

BAKED PEARS WITH CINNAMON, GREEK YOGURT AND TOASTED SEEDS

🔔 1 serving 🟢 25 min 🟢 Oven

INGREDIENTS:

1 small ripe pear, halved and cored (100g / ~3.5oz)
1/3 cup plain Greek yogurt, low-fat (80g / ~2.8oz)
1 tsp olive oil (5ml / ~0.17oz)
1/2 tsp ground cinnamon (1g / ~0.036oz)
1 tbsp mixed seeds (sunflower, pumpkin) (10g / ~0.35oz)

Also needed (not counted as main):
1/2 tsp low-carb sweetener (2g / ~0.07oz)
A few mint leaves for garnish (optional)

INSTRUCTIONS:

1. Preheat the oven to 375°F (190°C).
2. Place pear halves on a small baking tray, drizzle with olive oil, and sprinkle with cinnamon and sweetener.
3. Bake for 18–20 minutes until soft and lightly caramelized.
4. Meanwhile, toast seeds in a dry skillet over medium heat for 2–3 minutes until golden.
5. Remove pears from oven and let cool slightly. Top with Greek yogurt and toasted seeds.
6. Garnish with mint if desired and serve warm or at room temperature.

■ *For variety, try topping with a few chopped walnuts or a dash of lemon zest.*

Nutritional Information (Per Serving): **Calories: 210 kcal | Protein: 9g | Fat: 9g | Carbs: 20g | Fiber: 5g | Net Carbs: 15g**

HONEY-SESAME PHYLLO ROLLS WITH CRUSHED ALMONDS

🔔 1 serving 🟢 25 min 🟢 Oven

INGREDIENTS:

1 sheet phyllo dough (25g / ~0.9oz)
1 tbsp crushed almonds (10g / ~0.35oz)
1 tsp sesame seeds (3g / ~0.1oz)
1 tsp honey (5g / ~0.17oz)
1 tsp olive oil (5ml / ~0.17oz)

Also needed (not counted as main):
1/4 tsp ground cinnamon (0.5g / ~0.02oz)
Low-carb sweetener for dusting (optional)

INSTRUCTIONS:

1. Preheat oven to 375°F (190°C).
2. Lay out the phyllo sheet and brush lightly with olive oil.
3. Sprinkle with almonds, sesame seeds, and a pinch of cinnamon. Drizzle with honey.
4. Roll tightly into a cigar shape and place seam-side down on a parchment-lined baking tray.
5. Brush with oil and bake 15 minutes until golden. Cool slightly, slice, and optionally dust with low-carb sweetener.

■ *You can replace almonds with pistachios for a floral twist.*

Nutritional Information (Per Serving): **Calories: 195 kcal | Protein: 8g | Fat: 9g | Carbs: 18g | Fiber: 4g | Net Carbs: 14g**

OLIVE OIL ORANGE LOAF WITH FIG CHUNKS AND ROSEMARY

🔔 1 serving   ● 30 min   ● Oven

INGREDIENTS:

1/4 cup almond flour (30g / ~1.1oz)
2 tbsp ricotta cheese (30g / ~1oz)
1 tbsp olive oil (15ml / ~0.5oz)
1 tbsp fresh orange juice (15ml / ~0.5oz)
1 tbsp chopped dried figs (15g / ~0.5oz)

Also needed (not counted as main):
1/2 tsp orange zest (1g / ~0.04oz)
1/4 tsp chopped fresh rosemary (0.5g / ~0.02oz)
1/4 tsp baking powder (1g / ~0.04oz)
Pinch of sea salt
Low carb sweetener to taste

INSTRUCTIONS:

1. Preheat oven to 350°F (175°C). Line a mini loaf pan or ramekin with parchment or lightly grease it.
2. In a bowl, mix almond flour, baking powder, orange zest, rosemary, and a pinch of salt.
3. In a separate bowl, whisk ricotta, olive oil, orange juice, and sweetener. Combine wet and dry ingredients.
4. Fold in chopped figs. Pour batter into prepared pan and smooth the top.
5. Bake 18–20 minutes until golden and a toothpick comes out clean. Cool before serving.

■ *For a twist, top with a few crushed pistachios or an extra hint of orange zest before baking.*

> *Nutritional Information (Per Serving):* **Calories: 210 kcal | Protein: 9g | Fat: 9g | Carbs: 14g | Fiber: 4g | Net Carbs: 10g**

WARM PLUM CRISP WITH ALMOND CRUMBLE AND VANILLA LABNEH

🔔 1 serving   ● 25 min   ● Oven

INGREDIENTS:

1 small ripe plum, sliced (100g / ~3.5oz)
1/2 tsp cinnamon (1g / ~0.04oz)
1/2 tbsp almond flour (6g / ~0.21oz)
1 tbsp chopped almonds (10g / ~0.35oz)
1/2 tbsp olive oil (7ml / ~0.24oz)
1/2 tbsp low carb sweetener (6g / ~0.21oz)
2 tbsp plain labneh (40g / ~1.4oz)
1/4 tsp vanilla extract (1ml / ~0.03oz)

Also needed:
Pinch of sea salt

INSTRUCTIONS:

1. Preheat oven to 375°F (190°C). Toss sliced plum with cinnamon and sweetener, place in a small ramekin.
2. In a bowl, mix almond flour, almonds, olive oil, and a pinch of salt. Spoon crumble over plums.
3. Bake for 15–18 minutes until bubbling and golden on top.
4. Mix labneh with vanilla and serve a spoonful over warm crisp.

■ *Chill labneh in advance for a creamier contrast to warm fruit.*

> *Nutritional Information (Per Serving):* **Calories: 200 kcal | Protein: 8g | Fat: 9g | Carbs: 16g | Fiber: 5g | Net Carbs: 11g**

CHAPTER 11: Sweet Bowls to Share

GREEK YOGURT MOUSSE WITH ROASTED GRAPES AND PISTACHIOS

🔔 1 serving   🟢 25 min   🟢 Oven

INGREDIENTS:

1/2 cup plain Greek yogurt, 2% (120g / ~4.2oz)
1/4 cup red seedless grapes (40g / ~1.4oz)
1 tbsp chopped pistachios (10g / ~0.35oz)
1/2 tbsp extra virgin olive oil (7ml / ~0.24oz)
1/2 tbsp low carb sweetener (6g / ~0.21oz)
1/4 tsp vanilla extract (1ml / ~0.03oz)

Also needed:
Pinch of sea salt

INSTRUCTIONS:

1. Preheat oven to 400°F (200°C). Toss grapes with olive oil and a pinch of salt. Roast for 12–15 minutes until slightly blistered.
2. In a bowl, whisk yogurt with vanilla and sweetener until fluffy.
3. Spoon mousse into a bowl, top with warm roasted grapes and sprinkle with chopped pistachios.

▪ *Chill the yogurt mixture before serving for a more mousse-like texture.*

Nutritional Information (Per Serving): **Calories: 200 kcal | Protein: 9g | Fat: 9g | Carbs: 14g | Fiber: 4g | Net Carbs: 10g**

CARDAMOM RICE PUDDING WITH ROSEWATER AND TOASTED NUTS

🔔 1 serving   🟢 30 min   🟢 Stovetop

INGREDIENTS:

1/4 cup cooked short-grain rice (60g / ~2.1oz)
1/2 cup unsweetened almond milk (120ml / ~4oz)
1/4 cup plain Greek yogurt, 2% (60g / ~2.1oz)
1 tbsp chopped toasted almonds or walnuts (10g / ~0.35oz)
1/2 tbsp low carb sweetener (6g / ~0.21oz)
1/4 tsp ground cardamom (0.5g / ~0.02oz)
1/4 tsp rosewater (1ml / ~0.03oz)

Also needed:
Pinch of sea salt

INSTRUCTIONS:

1. In a saucepan, combine rice, almond milk, sweetener, cardamom, and a pinch of salt. Simmer over low heat for 10–12 minutes, stirring until thickened.
2. Remove from heat and stir in rosewater and yogurt until creamy.
3. Serve warm or chilled topped with toasted nuts.

▪ *For extra flavor, garnish with orange zest or a dusting of cinnamon.*

Nutritional Information (Per Serving): **Calories: 215 kcal | Protein: 8g | Fat: 8g | Carbs: 17g | Fiber: 5g | Net Carbs: 12g**

QUINOA PORRIDGE WITH PEARS, POMEGRANATE AND MINT

🛎 1 serving ● 20 min ● Stovetop

INGREDIENTS:

1/4 cup cooked quinoa (60g / ~2.1oz)
1/4 ripe pear, diced (50g / ~1.8oz)
2 tbsp pomegranate seeds (20g / ~0.7oz)
1/2 cup unsweetened almond milk (120ml / ~4oz)
1/2 tbsp low carb sweetener (6g / ~0.21oz)
1/2 tbsp chopped fresh mint (2g / ~0.07oz)

Also needed (not counted as main):
Pinch of cinnamon or cardamom

INSTRUCTIONS:

1. Add quinoa and almond milk to a small saucepan.
2. Simmer over medium heat for 5–7 min, stirring occasionally, until the mixture thickens slightly.
3. Stir in sweetener and a pinch of cinnamon. Remove from heat and let sit 2 min.
4. Transfer to a serving bowl and top with diced pear, pomegranate seeds, and mint.

■ *Chill before serving for a refreshing summer variation.*

Nutritional Information (Per Serving): **Calories: 210 kcal | Protein: 9g | Fat: 8g | Carbs: 20g | Fiber: 5g | Net Carbs: 15g**

CHIA PUDDING WITH ALMOND MILK, DATES AND CRUSHED WALNUTS

🛎 1 serving ● 10 min (plus chilling) ● No-Cook

INGREDIENTS:

3 tbsp chia seeds (30g / ~1.1oz)
1/2 cup unsweetened almond milk (120ml / ~4oz)
1 small Medjool date, finely chopped (15g / ~0.5oz)
1 tbsp crushed walnuts (7g / ~0.25oz)
1/2 tbsp low carb sweetener (6g / ~0.21oz)

Also needed (not counted as main):
Pinch of sea salt

INSTRUCTIONS:

1. In a small bowl, whisk chia seeds, almond milk, sweetener, and sea salt until well combined.
2. Let stand for 5 min, then stir again to prevent clumping.
3. Cover and refrigerate for 1–2 hours until thick and creamy.
4. Top with chopped date and crushed walnuts before serving.

■ *For extra creaminess, stir in 1 tbsp Greek yogurt before chilling.*

Nutritional Information (Per Serving): **Calories: 215 kcal | Protein: 8g | Fat: 9g | Carbs: 18g | Fiber: 5g | Net Carbs: 13g**

RICOTTA CREAM WITH SAUTÉED APPLES AND CINNAMON OIL

🔔 1 serving 🟢 15 min 🍃 Stovetop

INGREDIENTS:

1/3 cup part-skim ricotta cheese (80g / ~2.8oz)
1/2 small apple, diced (60g / ~2.1oz)
1/2 tbsp olive oil (8ml / ~0.28oz)
1/2 tbsp low carb sweetener (6g / ~0.21oz)
1/4 tsp ground cinnamon (0.5g / ~0.018oz)

Also needed (not counted as main):
Pinch of sea salt

INSTRUCTIONS:

1. In a skillet, heat olive oil over medium. Add diced apple and sauté for 4–5 minutes until softened and golden.
2. Sprinkle with cinnamon and a pinch of salt, stir gently, then remove from heat.
3. In a small bowl, whisk ricotta with sweetener until smooth and airy.
4. Spoon the ricotta cream into a bowl, top with warm cinnamon apples, and drizzle with any oil left in the pan.

▪ Add a few crushed walnuts or mint leaves for texture and brightness.

> *Nutritional Information (Per Serving):* **Calories: 210 kcal | Protein: 9g | Fat: 9g | Carbs: 19g | Fiber: 4g | Net Carbs: 15g**

COUSCOUS DESSERT BOWL WITH DRIED FRUITS AND ORANGE WATER

🔔 1 serving 🟢 20 min 🍃 Stovetop

INGREDIENTS:

3 tbsp dry whole wheat couscous (30g / ~1oz)
1/2 cup hot water (120ml / ~4oz)
1 tbsp raisins or chopped dried apricots (15g / ~0.5oz)
1/2 tsp orange blossom water (2.5ml / ~0.08oz)
1/2 tbsp low carb sweetener (6g / ~0.21oz)

Also needed (not counted as main):
1/2 tsp olive oil (2.5ml / ~0.08oz), pinch of cinnamon

INSTRUCTIONS:

1. Place couscous in a bowl and pour over hot water. Cover and let sit for 5–6 minutes.
2. Fluff couscous with a fork, then stir in dried fruit, sweetener, cinnamon, orange blossom water, and olive oil.
3. Let cool slightly and serve warm or chilled.

▪ For extra protein, add a spoonful of Greek yogurt on top.

> *Nutritional Information (Per Serving):* **Calories: 220 kcal | Protein: 8g | Fat: 8g | Carbs: 26g | Fiber: 5g | Net Carbs: 21g**

LABNEH WITH FRESH BERRIES, OLIVE OIL AND CRUSHED HAZELNUTS

🔔 1 serving ● 5 min ● No-Cook

INGREDIENTS:

1/3 cup labneh (75g / ~2.6oz)
1/4 cup mixed fresh berries (60g / ~2.1oz)
1 tbsp crushed hazelnuts, toasted (8g / ~0.28oz)
1 tsp olive oil (5ml / ~0.17oz)
1/2 tsp low carb sweetener (3g / ~0.1oz)

Also needed (not counted as main):
Pinch of sea salt

INSTRUCTIONS:

1. Spoon the labneh into a shallow serving bowl and use the back of a spoon to spread it into a gentle swirl.
2. Arrange the fresh berries on top, distributing them evenly.
3. Sprinkle the toasted crushed hazelnuts over the berries.
4. Drizzle with olive oil, then lightly dust with the low-carb sweetener.
5. Finish with a small pinch of sea salt to balance the flavors and serve immediately.

■ *Use seasonal berries like blackberries or red currants for a Mediterranean flair.*

> *Nutritional Information (Per Serving):* **Calories: 200 kcal** | Protein: 9g | Fat: 9g | Carbs: 17g | Fiber: 4g | Net Carbs: 13g

WARM MILLET PUDDING WITH FIGS, HONEY AND LEMON PEEL

🔔 1 serving ● 25 min ● Stovetop

INGREDIENTS:

3 tbsp millet (30g / ~1oz)
3/4 cup unsweetened almond milk (180ml / ~6oz)
1 dried fig, chopped (15g / ~0.5oz)
1/2 tsp lemon zest (1g / ~0.04oz)
1 tsp honey (7g / ~0.25oz)

Also needed (not counted as main):
Pinch of cinnamon, optional

INSTRUCTIONS:

1. In a small saucepan, combine millet and almond milk. Bring to a gentle simmer over medium heat.
2. Stir in the chopped fig and lemon zest. Reduce heat to low and cook uncovered for 18–20 minutes, stirring occasionally, until the millet is soft and the pudding has thickened.
3. Once cooked, remove from heat and let it rest for a minute.
4. Transfer to a serving bowl. Drizzle with honey and sprinkle a pinch of cinnamon if desired.

■ *Swap fig for chopped dates or apricots for variation.*

> *Nutritional Information (Per Serving):* **Calories: 215 kcal** | Protein: 9g | Fat: 8g | Carbs: 28g | Fiber: 5g | Net Carbs: 23g

CHAPTER 12: Chilled & Frozen Family Sweets

FROZEN YOGURT BARK WITH STRAWBERRIES AND SUNFLOWER SEEDS

🔔 1 serving   🟢 10 min (+ freeze time)   🌿 No-Cook

INGREDIENTS:

1/2 cup plain Greek yogurt (120g / ~4.2oz)
1/4 cup diced strawberries (40g / ~1.4oz)
1 tbsp sunflower seeds (10g / ~0.35oz)
1/2 tsp lemon zest (1g / ~0.035oz)
1/2 tsp low carb sweetener (2g / ~0.07oz)

Also needed:
Parchment paper, freezer-safe tray

INSTRUCTIONS:

1. Line a small tray with parchment paper.
2. In a bowl, mix Greek yogurt with sweetener and lemon zest until smooth.
3. Spread the mixture evenly on the tray to 1/4-inch thickness.
4. Top with strawberries and sunflower seeds, pressing lightly.
5. Freeze for 2–3 hours until firm, then break into pieces and serve immediately or store frozen.

▪ *For variation, try topping with blueberries or crushed pistachios.*

> *Nutritional Information (Per Serving):* **Calories: 200 kcal | Protein: 9g | Fat: 8g | Carbs: 16g | Fiber: 4g | Net Carbs: 12g**

HONEY-LEMON LABNEH CHEESECAKE CUPS WITH SESAME CRUST

🔔 1 serving   🟢 20 min   🌿 No-Bake

INGREDIENTS:

1/4 cup labneh (60g / ~2.1oz)
1 tbsp cream cheese (15g / ~0.5oz)
1/2 tbsp honey (10g / ~0.35oz)
1/2 tsp lemon juice (2.5ml / ~0.08oz)
1 tbsp ground sesame seeds (10g / ~0.35oz)

Also needed:
1 tbsp almond flour (10g / ~0.35oz), pinch of sea salt

INSTRUCTIONS:

1. Mix sesame seeds, almond flour, and a pinch of salt in a small bowl. Press into the bottom of a silicone muffin cup.
2. In another bowl, whisk labneh, cream cheese, honey, and lemon juice until smooth.
3. Spoon over the crust and smooth the top.
4. Chill in the fridge for 20 minutes or until firm.

▪ *Top with a sliver of fresh fig or sprinkle of lemon zest before serving.*

> *Nutritional Information (Per Serving):* **Calories: 215 kcal | Protein: 8g | Fat: 9g | Carbs: 15g | Fiber: 5g | Net Carbs: 10g**

ROSEWATER YOGURT POPSICLES WITH POMEGRANATE SEEDS

🔔 1 serving   🟢 10 min + freezing   ❄ Freezer

INGREDIENTS:

1/2 cup plain Greek yogurt, 2% fat (120g / ~4.2oz)
1 tbsp pomegranate seeds (10g / ~0.35oz)
1 tsp rosewater (5ml / ~0.17oz)
1/2 tbsp low carb sweetener (6g / ~0.21oz)
1 tsp lemon zest (2g / ~0.07oz)

Also needed (not counted as main):
Popsicle mold or silicone ice cube tray

INSTRUCTIONS:

1. In a small bowl, whisk Greek yogurt with rosewater, lemon zest, and low carb sweetener until smooth.
2. Gently fold in pomegranate seeds.
3. Spoon the mixture into a popsicle mold. Tap the mold lightly to remove air bubbles.
4. Freeze for at least 3–4 hours or until solid.
5. To serve, run warm water over the mold for a few seconds to release the popsicle.

■ *You can swap pomegranate for chopped berries if desired.*

Nutritional Information (Per Serving): **Calories: 190 kcal | Protein: 9g | Fat: 7g | Carbs: 13g | Fiber: 4g | Net Carbs: 9g**

ALMOND MILK ICE CREAM WITH CRUSHED APRICOTS & CARDAMOM

🔔 1 serving   🟢 20 min + freezing   ❄ Freezer

INGREDIENTS:

1/2 cup unsweetened almond milk (120ml / ~4.2oz)
2 tbsp part-skim ricotta cheese (30g / ~1oz)
1 dried apricot, finely chopped (10g / ~0.35oz)
1/4 tsp ground cardamom (0.5g / ~0.018oz)
1 tbsp low carb sweetener (12g / ~0.42oz)

Also needed (not counted as main):
Small freezer-safe bowl or ramekin

INSTRUCTIONS:

1. Blend almond milk, ricotta, cardamom, and low carb sweetener in a small blender until smooth and creamy.
2. Stir in the finely chopped dried apricot, then pour the mixture into a freezer-safe ramekin or shallow bowl.
3. Freeze for 2–3 hours. For a softer texture, stir the mixture once halfway through freezing.
4. Let sit at room temperature for 2 minutes before serving for easier scooping.

■ *Top with chopped pistachios for a crunchy finish, if you like.*

Nutritional Information (Per Serving): **Calories: 210 kcal | Protein: 9g | Fat: 7g | Carbs: 15g | Fiber: 4g | Net Carbs: 11g**

FROZEN BANANA HALVES WITH DARK CHOCOLATE & NUTS

🔔 1 serving   🟢 10 min + freezing   ❄ Freezer

INGREDIENTS:

1/2 medium banana, halved lengthwise (60g / ~2.1oz)
1 oz dark chocolate, 85% cocoa, chopped (28g / ~1oz)
1 tbsp chopped almonds or walnuts (8g / ~0.28oz)

Also needed (not counted as main):
Parchment paper

INSTRUCTIONS:

1. Gently melt the dark chocolate in a heat-safe bowl set over simmering water or microwave in 20-second bursts, stirring between each.
2. Line a small tray with parchment paper. Dip each banana half into the melted chocolate or spoon it evenly on top.
3. Sprinkle chopped nuts over the chocolate while still wet.
4. Place the coated bananas on the tray and freeze for 1–2 hours until fully firm.
5. Let sit at room temperature for 2 minutes to slightly soften before serving.

▮ *For a flavor twist, add a pinch of sea salt or a sprinkle of cinnamon before freezing.*

> *Nutritional Information (Per Serving):* **Calories: 200 kcal | Protein: 8g | Fat: 9g | Carbs: 19g | Fiber: 5g | Net Carbs: 14g**

SEMIFREDDO WITH TOASTED ALMONDS & ORANGE RIBBONS

🔔 1 serving   🟢 20 min + freezing   ❄ Freezer

INGREDIENTS:

1/4 cup part-skim ricotta (60g / ~2.1oz)
1 tbsp plain Greek yogurt, 2% (15g / ~0.5oz)
1 tbsp chopped toasted almonds (8g / ~0.28oz)
1 tsp orange zest (2g / ~0.07oz)
1 tbsp low carb sweetener (12g / ~0.42oz)

Also needed (not counted as main):
1 tsp orange juice (5ml / ~0.17oz), pinch of sea salt

INSTRUCTIONS:

1. In a small bowl, combine ricotta, yogurt, orange zest, sweetener, orange juice, and a pinch of sea salt. Mix until smooth and creamy.
2. Gently fold in the toasted almonds. Spoon the mixture into a lined ramekin or silicone mold, smoothing the top.
3. Freeze for 2–3 hours until firm but slightly soft in the center.
4. Remove from freezer and let rest 2–3 minutes. Serve with extra zest or chopped almonds if desired.

▮ *Use a microplane to get thin orange ribbons for decoration before freezing.*

> *Nutritional Information (Per Serving):* **Calories: 210 kcal | Protein: 9g | Fat: 9g | Carbs: 13g | Fiber: 4g | Net Carbs: 9g**

CHAPTER 13: Fruit-Forward Mediterranean Finishes

GRILLED PEACHES WITH BASIL AND BALSAMIC REDUCTION

🔔 1 serving   ● 15 min   🍃 Grill

INGREDIENTS:

1 medium peach, halved and pitted (150g / ~5.3oz)
1 oz low-fat ricotta cheese (30g / ~1.1oz)
1 tsp extra virgin olive oil (5ml / ~0.17oz)
1 tsp balsamic vinegar (5ml / ~0.17oz)
2–3 fresh basil leaves, sliced (1g / ~0.035oz)

Also needed (not counted as main):
Pinch of sea salt
Optional: low carb sweetener (1/4 tsp / 1g) if peach isn't fully ripe

INSTRUCTIONS:

1. Heat grill pan over medium-high and lightly brush peach halves with olive oil.
2. Grill cut-side down for 2–3 minutes until charred and tender.
3. In a small pan, simmer balsamic vinegar until thickened. Stir in sweetener if using.
4. Top grilled peaches with ricotta, balsamic, basil, and sea salt.

■ A touch of lemon zest in the ricotta adds freshness and balance.

> *Nutritional Information (Per Serving):* **Calories: 205 kcal | Protein: 9g | Fat: 8g | Carbs: 20g | Fiber: 5g | Net Carbs: 15g**

WATERMELON WEDGES WITH FETA, MINT AND HONEY DRIZZLE

🔔 1 serving   ● 10 min   ❄ No Cook

INGREDIENTS:

1 cup watermelon, cut into wedges (150g / ~5.3oz)
1 oz feta cheese, crumbled (30g / ~1.1oz)
1 tsp extra virgin olive oil (5ml / ~0.17oz)
1/2 tsp raw honey (3g / ~0.1oz)
1 tbsp fresh mint, finely chopped (2g / ~0.07oz)

Also needed (not counted as main):
Pinch of sea salt and black pepper

INSTRUCTIONS:

1. Arrange watermelon wedges on a serving plate.
2. Crumble feta evenly over the top and drizzle with olive oil and honey.
3. Sprinkle with chopped mint, sea salt, and black pepper.
4. Serve immediately while cold and fresh.

■ For a zestier twist, add a squeeze of lime juice or a few chili flakes.

> *Nutritional Information (Per Serving):* **Calories: 190 kcal | Protein: 8g | Fat: 9g | Carbs: 17g | Fiber: 4g | Net Carbs: 13g**

CITRUS SALAD WITH TOASTED PISTACHIOS AND YOGURT SWIRL

🔔 1 serving   🟢 15 min   🟢 No Cook

INGREDIENTS:

1 orange, peeled and sliced (130g / ~4.6oz)
2 tbsp low-fat Greek yogurt (30g / ~1.1oz)
1 tbsp pistachios, toasted and chopped (10g / ~0.35oz)
1 tsp extra virgin olive oil (5ml / ~0.17oz)
1/4 tsp ground cardamom (0.5g / ~0.018oz)

Also needed (not counted as main):
Pinch of sea salt
Optional: low carb sweetener (1/4 tsp / 1g) for extra balance

INSTRUCTIONS:

1. Toast pistachios in a dry skillet over medium heat for 2–3 minutes until fragrant.
2. Arrange orange slices on a plate and dollop with Greek yogurt.
3. Drizzle with olive oil, sprinkle toasted pistachios and cardamom on top.
4. Add a pinch of sea salt and sweetener if desired. Serve immediately.

▪ *Try mixing blood orange and navel slices for added flavor and color contrast.*

> *Nutritional Information (Per Serving):* **Calories: 210 kcal | Protein: 9g | Fat: 9g | Carbs: 20g | Fiber: 5g | Net Carbs: 15g**

CARAMELIZED ORANGES WITH OLIVE OIL AND CINNAMON

🔔 1 serving   🟢 20 min   🟢 Stovetop

INGREDIENTS:

1 orange, peeled and cut into rounds (130g / ~4.6oz)
1 tbsp low-fat ricotta (15g / ~0.5oz)
1 tsp extra virgin olive oil (5ml / ~0.17oz)
1/4 tsp cinnamon (0.5g / ~0.018oz)
1/4 tsp low carb sweetener (1g / ~0.035oz)

Also needed (not counted as main):
Pinch of sea salt

INSTRUCTIONS:

1. Heat olive oil in a nonstick skillet over medium heat.
2. Add orange slices and cook 1–2 minutes per side until lightly golden.
3. Sprinkle with cinnamon and low carb sweetener. Sauté for another 1–2 minutes.
4. Serve warm with a small spoonful of ricotta and sea salt to finish.

▪ *A splash of orange blossom water can elevate the aroma beautifully.*

> *Nutritional Information (Per Serving):* **Calories: 195 kcal | Protein: 8g | Fat: 8g | Carbs: 18g | Fiber: 4g | Net Carbs: 14g**

ROASTED APPLE RINGS WITH LABNEH AND ALMOND CRUST

🔔 1 serving ● 25 min ● Oven

INGREDIENTS:

1 small apple, cored and sliced into 3 rings (100g / ~3.5oz)
2 tbsp labneh (40g / ~1.4oz)
1 tbsp finely chopped almonds, toasted (10g / ~0.35oz)
1/2 tsp extra virgin olive oil (2.5ml / ~0.08oz)
1/4 tsp cinnamon (0.5g / ~0.018oz)

Also needed (not counted as main):
Pinch of sea salt
Optional: low carb sweetener (1/4 tsp / 1g) for a sweeter touch

INSTRUCTIONS:

1. Preheat the oven to 375°F (190°C).
2. Brush apple rings with olive oil and place on a parchment-lined baking tray.
3. Roast for 15–18 minutes until golden and soft.
4. Spread labneh over each warm ring, sprinkle with almonds and cinnamon.
5. Finish with a pinch of sea salt and sweetener if needed. Serve warm or room temp.

■ For a crunchier finish, broil the apples for the last 2 minutes.

> *Nutritional Information (Per Serving):* **Calories: 215 kcal | Protein: 9g | Fat: 9g | Carbs: 20g | Fiber: 5g | Net Carbs: 15g**

BAKED GRAPEFRUIT HALVES WITH HONEY AND ROSEMARY SUGAR

🔔 1 serving ● 20 min ● Oven

INGREDIENTS:

1/2 large grapefruit (150g / ~5.3oz)
2 tbsp low-fat Greek yogurt (30g / ~1.1oz)
1/2 tsp raw honey (3g / ~0.1oz)
1/4 tsp finely chopped fresh rosemary (0.5g / ~0.018oz)
1/4 tsp low carb sweetener (1g / ~0.035oz)

Also needed (not counted as main):
Pinch of sea salt

INSTRUCTIONS:

1. Preheat oven to 400°F (200°C).
2. In a small bowl, mix rosemary, low carb sweetener, and a pinch of sea salt.
3. Place grapefruit half cut-side up in a baking dish. Drizzle with honey and sprinkle rosemary sugar over the top.
4. Bake for 10–12 minutes until surface is golden and bubbly.
5. Serve warm with a spoonful of Greek yogurt on the side.

■ For extra aroma, add a tiny drop of vanilla extract to the yogurt.

> *Nutritional Information (Per Serving):* **Calories: 200 kcal | Protein: 9g | Fat: 7g | Carbs: 19g | Fiber: 4g | Net Carbs: 15g**

FIG AND POMEGRANATE COMPOTE WITH RICOTTA CLOUDS

🔔 1 serving   ● 15 min   🌿 Stovetop

INGREDIENTS:

2 fresh figs, chopped (80g / ~2.8oz)
2 tbsp pomegranate seeds (20g / ~0.7oz)
2 tbsp low-fat ricotta cheese (30g / ~1.1oz)
1/2 tsp lemon zest (1g / ~0.035oz)
1/4 tsp low carb sweetener (1g / ~0.035oz)

Also needed (not counted as main):
Pinch of sea salt
Optional: 1 tbsp water (15ml / ~0.5oz) for loosening compote

INSTRUCTIONS:

1. In a small pan, combine figs, pomegranate seeds, lemon zest, sweetener, and a splash of water. Simmer over medium heat for 5–7 minutes until softened.
2. Let cool slightly, then spoon into a bowl.
3. Top with dollops of ricotta and a tiny pinch of sea salt. Serve warm or chilled.

■ *For added flavor, stir a few fresh mint leaves into the compote just before serving.*

> **Nutritional Information (Per Serving):** Calories: 200 kcal | Protein: 9g | Fat: 7g | Carbs: 21g | Fiber: 5g | Net Carbs: 16g

PEAR AND PLUM SKILLET WITH CRUSHED WALNUTS AND OAT CRUST

🔔 1 serving   ● 25 min   🌿 Stovetop

INGREDIENTS:

1/2 small pear, sliced (60g / ~2.1oz)
1/2 small plum, sliced (60g / ~2.1oz)
1 tbsp rolled oats (8g / ~0.3oz)
1 tbsp walnuts, crushed (8g / ~0.3oz)
2 tbsp low-fat Greek yogurt (30g / ~1.1oz)
1 tsp olive oil (5ml / ~0.17oz)

Also needed (not counted as main):
1/4 tsp cinnamon (0.5g / ~0.018oz)
Pinch of sea salt

INSTRUCTIONS:

1. Heat olive oil in a skillet over medium heat. Add pear and plum slices, sprinkle with cinnamon and a pinch of salt.
2. Sauté 5–6 minutes until softened and lightly golden.
3. Sprinkle oats and walnuts on top, cook 2–3 minutes more until crisp.
4. Serve warm with a spoonful of Greek yogurt.

■ *To enhance crunch, toast the oats and walnuts separately before adding.*

> **Nutritional Information (Per Serving):** Calories: 215 kcal | Protein: 9g | Fat: 9g | Carbs: 22g | Fiber: 5g | Net Carbs: 17g

DINNER: CHAPTER 14: Family Classics with a Mediterranean Touch

LEMON-GARLIC ROAST CHICKEN WITH POTATOES AND GREEN BEANS

🔔 1 serving   ● 30 min   ● Oven

INGREDIENTS:

1 skinless chicken thigh, bone-in (120g / ~4.2oz)
1/2 cup baby potatoes, halved (80g / ~2.8oz)
1/2 cup green beans, trimmed (60g / ~2.1oz)
1 tbsp olive oil (15ml / ~0.5oz)
1 tbsp lemon juice (15ml / ~0.5oz)

Also needed (not counted as main):
1 garlic clove, minced (3g / ~0.1oz)
1/2 tsp dried oregano (1g / ~0.036oz)
Salt and black pepper to taste

INSTRUCTIONS:

1. Preheat oven to 400°F (200°C).
2. In a bowl, toss chicken, potatoes, and green beans with olive oil, lemon juice, garlic, oregano, salt, and pepper.
3. Place everything in a baking dish. Roast for 25–28 minutes, flipping vegetables once, until chicken is golden and cooked through.
4. Serve warm with pan juices on top.

■ Add a few lemon slices to the pan for extra aroma and color.

> *Nutritional Information (Per Serving):* **Calories: 520 kcal | Protein: 24g | Fat: 16g | Carbs: 27g | Fiber: 8g | Net Carbs: 19g**

HERBED LAMB CHOPS WITH ROASTED CARROTS AND MINT YOGURT

🔔 1 serving   ● 30 min   ● Oven & Stovetop

INGREDIENTS:

1 small lamb chop, bone-in (120g / ~4.2oz)
1/2 cup carrots, sliced (70g / ~2.5oz)
2 tbsp low-fat Greek yogurt (30g / ~1.1oz)
1 tbsp chopped fresh mint (2g / ~0.07oz)
1 tbsp olive oil (15ml / ~0.5oz)

Also needed (not counted as main):
1/2 tsp dried rosemary or thyme (1g / ~0.036oz)
Salt and black pepper to taste

INSTRUCTIONS:

1. Preheat oven to 400°F (200°C). Toss carrots with 1/2 tbsp olive oil, salt, pepper, and roast for 20–25 minutes.
2. Meanwhile, season lamb with herbs, salt, and pepper. Heat 1/2 tbsp olive oil in a skillet and sear lamb 2–3 minutes per side until golden and just cooked through.
3. Mix yogurt with chopped mint and a pinch of salt. Serve lamb with carrots and mint yogurt.

■ Let the lamb rest 2 minutes before serving for juicier meat.

> *Nutritional Information (Per Serving):* **Calories: 540 kcal | Protein: 22g | Fat: 18g | Carbs: 22g | Fiber: 7g | Net Carbs: 15g**

TURKEY MEATBALLS IN TOMATO-OLIVE SAUCE WITH COUSCOUS

🔔 1 serving   ● 30 min   ● Stovetop

INGREDIENTS:

4 oz ground turkey (115g / ~4oz)
1/2 cup canned crushed tomatoes (120g / ~4.2oz)
1 tbsp chopped green olives (10g / ~0.35oz)
1/4 cup whole wheat couscous, dry (40g / ~1.4oz)
1 tbsp olive oil (15ml / ~0.5oz)

Also needed (not counted as main):
1 garlic clove, minced (3g / ~0.1oz)
1/2 tsp dried basil or oregano (1g / ~0.036oz)
Salt and black pepper to taste

INSTRUCTIONS:

1. In a bowl, mix ground turkey with a pinch of salt and pepper. Form into 4 small meatballs.
2. Heat 1/2 tbsp olive oil in a skillet and brown meatballs on all sides for 6–7 minutes.
3. Add crushed tomatoes, garlic, olives, and herbs. Simmer covered for 10 minutes.
4. Meanwhile, cook couscous with 1/2 tbsp olive oil and a pinch of salt according to package instructions (typically 5 min resting in hot water).
5. Serve meatballs and sauce over couscous.

■ Add fresh parsley or lemon zest to the couscous for a bright finish.

Nutritional Information (Per Serving): **Calories: 540 kcal | Protein: 24g | Fat: 16g | Carbs: 30g | Fiber: 8g | Net Carbs: 22g**

ONE-PAN CHICKEN THIGHS WITH SWEET POTATO AND RED ONION

🔔 1 serving   ● 30 min   ● Oven

INGREDIENTS:

1 boneless, skinless chicken thigh (120g / ~4.2oz)
1/2 small sweet potato, diced (90g / ~3.2oz)
1/4 medium red onion, sliced (40g / ~1.4oz)
1 tbsp olive oil (15ml / ~0.5oz)
1 tsp fresh rosemary or thyme, chopped (2g / ~0.07oz)

Also needed (not counted as main):
Salt and black pepper to taste

INSTRUCTIONS:

1. Preheat oven to 400°F (200°C).
2. Toss sweet potato and red onion with 1/2 tbsp olive oil, herbs, salt, and pepper. Spread on a baking tray.
3. Rub chicken thigh with remaining olive oil, salt, and pepper. Place on the tray with vegetables.
4. Roast for 25–28 minutes, flipping vegetables once, until chicken is golden and cooked through.
5. Serve warm with tray juices drizzled on top.

■ Add a squeeze of lemon over the finished dish to lift the flavors.

Nutritional Information (Per Serving): **Calories: 510 kcal | Protein: 23g | Fat: 17g | Carbs: 26g | Fiber: 7g | Net Carbs: 19g**

BAKED FISH FILLETS WITH FENNEL, TOMATO AND DILL CRUST

🔔 1 serving   ● 25 min   ● Oven

INGREDIENTS:

1 white fish fillet (cod or haddock) (150g / ~5.3oz)
1/2 cup cherry tomatoes, halved (80g / ~2.8oz)
1/3 cup fennel bulb, thinly sliced (50g / ~1.8oz)
1 tbsp olive oil (15ml / ~0.5oz)
1 tbsp chopped fresh dill (3g / ~0.1oz)

Also needed (not counted as main):
1 garlic clove, finely minced (3g / ~0.1oz)
Salt and pepper to taste

INSTRUCTIONS:

1. Preheat oven to 375°F (190°C).
2. Toss sliced fennel and cherry tomatoes with 1/2 tbsp olive oil, garlic, salt, and pepper. Spread on a baking tray.
3. Place fish on top, drizzle with remaining olive oil, and sprinkle dill over the fillet.
4. Bake for 15–18 minutes until the fish flakes easily and the vegetables are tender.
5. Serve warm with pan juices spooned over.

■ *Add a splash of lemon juice just before serving to brighten the flavor.*

Nutritional Information (Per Serving): **Calories: 495 kcal | Protein: 25g | Fat: 16g | Carbs: 18g | Fiber: 7g | Net Carbs: 11g**

STUFFED BELL PEPPERS WITH BROWN RICE, CHICKPEAS AND FETA

🔔 1 serving   ● 30 min   ● Oven

INGREDIENTS:

1 medium bell pepper, halved and deseeded (120g / ~4.2oz)
1/4 cup cooked brown rice (50g / ~1.8oz)
1/4 cup canned chickpeas, drained (40g / ~1.4oz)
2 tbsp crumbled feta cheese (30g / ~1.1oz)
1 tbsp olive oil (15ml / ~0.5oz)

Also needed (not counted as main):
1/2 tsp dried oregano (1g / ~0.036oz)
Salt and black pepper to taste

INSTRUCTIONS:

1. Preheat oven to 400°F (200°C).
2. In a bowl, mix brown rice, chickpeas, feta, oregano, 1/2 tbsp olive oil, salt, and pepper.
3. Fill each bell pepper half with the mixture and drizzle with remaining olive oil.
4. Place in a small baking dish and bake for 20–22 minutes until the pepper is tender and the filling golden.

■ *Add a spoonful of Greek yogurt or chopped fresh mint before serving for extra brightness.*

Nutritional Information (Per Serving): **Calories: 540 kcal | Protein: 19g | Fat: 17g | Carbs: 29g | Fiber: 8g | Net Carbs: 21g**

BEEF & EGGPLANT CASSEROLE WITH GARLIC AND CINNAMON

🔔 1 serving   ● 30 min   🌿 Stovetop & Oven

INGREDIENTS:

4 oz lean ground beef (115g / ~4oz)
1/2 small eggplant, diced (100g / ~3.5oz)
1/3 cup crushed tomatoes (80g / ~2.8oz)
1 tbsp olive oil (15ml / ~0.5oz)
1/4 tsp ground cinnamon (0.5g / ~0.018oz)

Also needed (not counted as main):
1 garlic clove, finely minced (3g / ~0.1oz)
Salt and black pepper to taste

INSTRUCTIONS:

1. Preheat oven to 375°F (190°C).
2. In a pan, heat 1/2 tbsp olive oil and sauté eggplant for 5–6 minutes until golden. Remove and set aside.
3. In the same pan, cook beef with garlic, cinnamon, salt, and pepper for 5 minutes until browned. Add tomatoes and simmer 5 more minutes.
4. Add eggplant and transfer to baking dish.
5. Drizzle remaining olive oil over the top and bake for 10 minutes until bubbling.

■ *Serve with chopped parsley or a spoonful of Greek yogurt for a creamy contrast.*

> *Nutritional Information (Per Serving):* **Calories: 510 kcal | Protein: 23g | Fat: 17g | Carbs: 19g | Fiber: 8g | Net Carbs: 11g**

ROASTED CHICKEN LEGS WITH LEMON RICE AND SPINACH

🔔 1 serving   ● 30 min   ● Oven & Stovetop

INGREDIENTS:

1 small chicken leg, skin-on (150g / ~5.3oz)
1/4 cup cooked brown rice (50g / ~1.8oz)
1 cup baby spinach (30g / ~1oz)
1 tbsp olive oil (15ml / ~0.5oz)
1 tbsp lemon juice (15ml / ~0.5oz)

Also needed (not counted as main):
1 garlic clove, minced (3g / ~0.1oz)
Salt and black pepper to taste

INSTRUCTIONS:

1. Preheat oven to 400°F (200°C). Season chicken with salt and pepper. Roast for 25–28 minutes until golden and juices run clear.
2. While roasting, heat 1/2 tbsp olive oil in a pan. Sauté garlic and spinach for 2–3 minutes until wilted.
3. Stir in brown rice and lemon juice, cooking for 2 more minutes.
4. Serve chicken leg over the lemon rice-spinach mix and drizzle with remaining olive oil.

■ *Add fresh dill or parsley for a herbaceous boost.*

> *Nutritional Information (Per Serving):* **Calories: 545 kcal | Protein: 24g | Fat: 16g | Carbs: 22g | Fiber: 7g | Net Carbs: 15g**

GRILLED SALMON WITH QUINOA, CUCUMBER AND YOGURT HERB SAUCE

🔔 1 serving ● 25 min ● Grill & Stovetop

INGREDIENTS:

1 salmon fillet (120g / ~4.2oz)
1/4 cup cooked quinoa (50g / ~1.8oz)
1/4 cup cucumber, diced (40g / ~1.4oz)
2 tbsp low-fat Greek yogurt (30g / ~1.1oz)
1 tbsp olive oil (15ml / ~0.5oz)

Also needed (not counted as main):
1 tbsp chopped fresh dill or parsley (2g / ~0.07oz)
1/2 tsp lemon juice (2ml / ~0.07oz)
Salt and pepper to taste

INSTRUCTIONS:

1. Heat grill pan over medium-high and brush salmon with 1/2 tbsp olive oil, salt, and pepper. Grill for 3–4 minutes per side.
2. Toss cooked quinoa with diced cucumber, lemon juice, and remaining olive oil.
3. Stir yogurt with fresh herbs, a pinch of salt, and serve as sauce.
4. Plate salmon over quinoa-cucumber salad and drizzle with yogurt herb sauce.

■ Add lemon zest to the yogurt for extra brightness.

Nutritional Information (Per Serving): **Calories: 525 kcal | Protein: 24g | Fat: 17g | Carbs: 20g | Fiber: 8g | Net Carbs: 12g**

BAKED PASTA WITH ZUCCHINI, TOMATOES AND PARMESAN CRUST

🔔 1 serving ● 30 min ● Oven

INGREDIENTS:

1/2 cup whole wheat penne, cooked (60g / ~2.1oz)
1/4 cup zucchini, diced (40g / ~1.4oz)
1/4 cup cherry tomatoes, halved (50g / ~1.8oz)
2 tbsp grated Parmesan (20g / ~0.7oz)
1 tbsp olive oil (15ml / ~0.5oz)

Also needed (not counted as main):
1 garlic clove, minced (3g / ~0.1oz)
1/2 tsp dried oregano (1g / ~0.036oz)
Salt and pepper to taste

INSTRUCTIONS:

1. Preheat oven to 375°F (190°C).
2. Sauté zucchini and garlic in 1/2 tbsp olive oil for 4–5 minutes.
3. In a bowl, mix cooked pasta with zucchini, cherry tomatoes, oregano, salt, and pepper.
4. Transfer to a small baking dish, sprinkle with Parmesan, drizzle with remaining olive oil.
5. Bake for 12–15 minutes until golden and bubbly.

■ Add a few basil leaves before serving for a fresh finish.

Nutritional Information (Per Serving): **Calories: 495 kcal | Protein: 19g | Fat: 15g | Carbs: 27g | Fiber: 9g | Net Carbs: 18g**

CHAPTER 15: Sheet Pans, Skillets & Casseroles

SHEET-PAN SHRIMP WITH CAULIFLOWER, BELL PEPPERS AND LEMON

🔔 1 serving ● 25 min ● Oven

INGREDIENTS:

4 oz raw shrimp, peeled and deveined (115g / ~4oz)
1 cup cauliflower florets (100g / ~3.5oz)
1/2 cup bell pepper, sliced (60g / ~2.1oz)
1 tbsp olive oil (15ml / ~0.5oz)
1 tbsp lemon juice (15ml / ~0.5oz)

Also needed (not counted as main):
1/2 tsp smoked paprika (1g / ~0.036oz)
1 garlic clove, minced (3g / ~0.1oz)
Salt and black pepper to taste

INSTRUCTIONS:

1. Preheat oven to 400°F (200°C).
2. Toss shrimp, cauliflower, and bell pepper with olive oil, lemon juice, garlic, paprika, salt, and pepper.
3. Spread on a parchment-lined sheet pan in a single layer.
4. Roast for 15–18 minutes until shrimp are pink and vegetables are tender.
5. Serve hot with extra lemon wedges if desired.

■ *Add a sprinkle of fresh parsley or chili flakes before serving for added flavor.*

> *Nutritional Information (Per Serving):* **Calories: 495 kcal | Protein: 24g | Fat: 15g | Carbs: 20g | Fiber: 8g | Net Carbs: 12g**

SKILLET TURKEY AND LENTILS WITH CARROT AND THYME

🔔 1 serving ● 30 min ● Stovetop

INGREDIENTS:

4 oz ground turkey (115g / ~4oz)
1/4 cup cooked green lentils (50g / ~1.8oz)
1/3 cup carrots, diced (40g / ~1.4oz)
1 tbsp olive oil (15ml / ~0.5oz)
1/2 tsp dried thyme (1g / ~0.036oz)

Also needed (not counted as main):
1 garlic clove, minced (3g / ~0.1oz)
Salt and black pepper to taste

INSTRUCTIONS:

1. Heat olive oil in a skillet over medium heat.
2. Add carrots and garlic, sauté for 3–4 minutes until softened.
3. Stir in ground turkey, season with salt, pepper, and thyme. Cook for 6–7 minutes until browned.
4. Add lentils and cook for another 5 minutes, stirring occasionally until warmed through.
5. Serve hot with a drizzle of olive oil and optional lemon zest.

■ *Add a handful of baby spinach at the end for color and added nutrients.*

> *Nutritional Information (Per Serving):* **Calories: 520 kcal | Protein: 23g | Fat: 16g | Carbs: 25g | Fiber: 9g | Net Carbs: 16g**

ONE-DISH CHICKEN AND ORZO WITH CHERRY TOMATOES & SPINACH

🔔 1 serving 🟢 25 min 🟢 Skillet

INGREDIENTS:

4 oz skinless chicken breast, diced (115g / ~4oz)
1/2 cup cooked whole wheat orzo (85g / ~3oz)
1/2 cup cherry tomatoes, halved (75g / ~2.6oz)
1 cup fresh spinach, loosely packed (30g / ~1oz)
1 tbsp extra virgin olive oil (15ml / ~0.5oz)

Also needed (not counted as main):
1 garlic clove, finely minced (3g / ~0.1oz)
1/2 tsp dried oregano (1g / ~0.035oz)
Salt and black pepper to taste
Squeeze of lemon (1 tsp / 5ml / ~0.17oz)

INSTRUCTIONS:

1. Heat olive oil in a nonstick skillet over medium heat. Add garlic and sauté for 30 seconds.
2. Add chicken, season with salt, pepper, and oregano, and cook for 5–6 minutes until golden and cooked through.
3. Stir in tomatoes and cook for 2 minutes until softened.
4. Add cooked orzo and spinach. Stir until spinach is wilted and orzo is warmed through, about 2–3 minutes.
5. Finish with a squeeze of lemon. Serve hot, garnished with extra oregano if desired.

▪ *For extra flavor, add a few torn fresh basil leaves or crumbled feta at the end.*

> *Nutritional Information (Per Serving):* **Calories: 495 kcal | Protein: 35g | Fat: 17g | Carbs: 27g | Fiber: 8g | Net Carbs: 19g**

FAMILY PAN RATATOUILLE WITH GOAT CHEESE & BASIL OIL

🔔 1 serving 🟢 30 min 🟢 Oven

INGREDIENTS:

1/4 small eggplant, cubed (80g / ~2.8oz)
1/4 zucchini, sliced (60g / ~2.1oz)
1/4 red bell pepper, chopped (50g / ~1.8oz)
1 oz goat cheese, crumbled (30g / ~1oz)
1 tbsp olive oil (15ml / ~0.5oz)

Also needed (not counted as main):
1 garlic clove, minced (3g / ~0.1oz)
1/2 tsp dried thyme (1g / ~0.035oz)
Salt and pepper to taste
Fresh basil leaves + 1 tsp olive oil for basil oil drizzle (5ml / ~0.17oz)

INSTRUCTIONS:

1. Preheat oven to 400°F (200°C).
2. In a mixing bowl, toss eggplant, zucchini, bell pepper, garlic, thyme, salt, and olive oil.
3. Spread mixture in a small baking dish or sheet pan. Roast for 20 minutes, stirring halfway.
4. Remove from oven, top with goat cheese, and drizzle with basil oil (blend fresh basil with olive oil).
5. Serve warm, garnished with extra basil if desired.

▪ *Add a handful of baby arugula before serving for a peppery twist.*

> *Nutritional Information (Per Serving):* **Calories: 470 kcal | Protein: 19g | Fat: 18g | Carbs: 26g | Fiber: 9g | Net Carbs: 17g**

SHRIMP AND CHICKPEA BAKE WITH ZUCCHINI & RED ONION

🔔 1 serving ● 25 min ● Oven

INGREDIENTS:

4 oz raw shrimp, peeled and deveined (115g / ~4oz)
1/2 cup canned chickpeas, rinsed and drained (80g / ~2.8oz)
1/2 small zucchini, sliced (75g / ~2.6oz)
1/4 small red onion, thinly sliced (30g / ~1oz)
1 tbsp olive oil (15ml / ~0.5oz)

Also needed (not counted as main):
1 garlic clove, finely minced (3g / ~0.1oz)
1/2 tsp smoked paprika (1g / ~0.035oz)
Salt and pepper to taste
Juice of 1/4 lemon (1 tsp / 5ml / ~0.17oz)

INSTRUCTIONS:

1. Preheat oven to 400°F (200°C).
2. Toss shrimp, chickpeas, zucchini, and red onion with olive oil, garlic, paprika, salt, and pepper.
3. Spread mixture in a single layer on a small sheet pan.
4. Bake for 15–18 minutes until shrimp are pink and vegetables are tender.
5. Drizzle with lemon juice and serve warm.

▪ Add a pinch of chili flakes for extra kick or top with chopped parsley before serving.

Nutritional Information (Per Serving): **Calories: 490 kcal | Protein: 25g | Fat: 17g | Carbs: 25g | Fiber: 8g | Net Carbs: 17g**

CASSEROLE OF WHITE BEANS, ROASTED PEPPERS & FETA CRUMBLE

🔔 1 serving ● 30 min ● Oven

INGREDIENTS:

1/2 cup canned white beans, rinsed and drained (90g / ~3.2oz)
1/4 cup roasted red peppers, chopped (60g / ~2.1oz)
1/4 small zucchini, diced (50g / ~1.8oz)
1 oz feta cheese, crumbled (30g / ~1oz)
1 tbsp olive oil (15ml / ~0.5oz)

Also needed (not counted as main):
1 garlic clove, minced (3g / ~0.1oz)
1/2 tsp dried oregano (1g / ~0.035oz)
Salt and pepper to taste

INSTRUCTIONS:

1. Preheat oven to 375°F (190°C).
2. In a bowl, mix beans, zucchini, red peppers, garlic, oregano, olive oil, salt, and pepper.
3. Transfer to a small casserole dish and top with crumbled feta.
4. Bake for 20–25 minutes until hot and feta is slightly golden.
5. Serve warm with a drizzle of extra olive oil if desired.

▪ Add a few fresh basil leaves after baking for a bright, herbal finish.

Nutritional Information (Per Serving): **Calories: 510 kcal | Protein: 19g | Fat: 18g | Carbs: 29g | Fiber: 9g | Net Carbs: 20g**

SALMON TRAY BAKE WITH SWEET POTATO, DILL & LEMON

🔔 1 serving ⏺ 25 min 🌿 Oven

INGREDIENTS:

4 oz salmon fillet, skinless (115g / ~4oz)
1/2 small sweet potato, sliced (90g / ~3.2oz)
1/2 small zucchini, sliced (60g / ~2.1oz)
1 tbsp olive oil (15ml / ~0.5oz)
1 tbsp fresh dill, chopped (2g / ~0.07oz)

Also needed (not counted as main):
Salt and pepper to taste
2 lemon slices (10g / ~0.35oz)
1 garlic clove, minced (3g / ~0.1oz)

INSTRUCTIONS:

1. Preheat oven to 400°F (200°C).
2. Toss sweet potato and zucchini with half the olive oil, salt, and garlic. Spread on a lined tray and roast for 10 minutes.
3. Add salmon fillet on top, drizzle with remaining oil, season with salt and pepper, and top with dill and lemon slices.
4. Roast for another 12–14 minutes until salmon is cooked through and flakes easily.
5. Serve warm with pan juices spooned over.

■ *For extra zest, grate a little lemon zest over the salmon before serving.*

> ***Nutritional Information (Per Serving):** Calories: 525 kcal | Protein: 24g | Fat: 18g | Carbs: 26g | Fiber: 8g | Net Carbs: 18g*

SKILLET LAMB & COUSCOUS WITH CUMIN & RAISINS

🔔 1 serving ⏺ 30 min 🌿 Skillet

INGREDIENTS:

3 oz ground lamb (85g / ~3oz)
1/3 cup cooked whole wheat couscous (65g / ~2.3oz)
1 tbsp raisins (10g / ~0.35oz)
1/4 small red onion, diced (25g / ~0.9oz)
1 tbsp olive oil (15ml / ~0.5oz)

Also needed (not counted as main):
1/2 tsp ground cumin (1g / ~0.035oz)
Salt and pepper to taste
1 tbsp chopped parsley (3g / ~0.1oz)
Squeeze of lemon (1 tsp / 5ml / ~0.17oz)

INSTRUCTIONS:

1. Heat olive oil in a skillet over medium heat. Add onion and sauté 2 minutes.
2. Add ground lamb, cumin, salt, and pepper. Cook for 6–8 minutes until browned and fully cooked.
3. Stir in couscous and raisins. Cook for 2 more minutes until warmed through.
4. Remove from heat, add parsley and a squeeze of lemon.

■ *Add a pinch of cinnamon for deeper Moroccan-inspired flavor.*

> ***Nutritional Information (Per Serving):** Calories: 495 kcal | Protein: 22g | Fat: 17g | Carbs: 28g | Fiber: 7g | Net Carbs: 21g*

MEDITERRANEAN SHEPHERD'S PIE WITH GROUND BEEF & EGGPLANT

🔔 1 serving   ● 30 min   ● Oven + Skillet

INGREDIENTS:

4 oz lean ground beef (115g / ~4oz)
1/2 small eggplant, diced (90g / ~3.2oz)
1/3 cup cooked mashed cauliflower (75g / ~2.6oz)
1/4 small onion, chopped (30g / ~1oz)
1 tbsp olive oil (15ml / ~0.5oz)

Also needed (not counted as main):
1 garlic clove, minced (3g / ~0.1oz)
1/2 tsp dried oregano (1g / ~0.035oz)
Salt and pepper to taste

INSTRUCTIONS:

1. Preheat oven to 375°F (190°C).
2. Heat olive oil in a skillet. Sauté onion and garlic for 2–3 minutes. Add beef and oregano; cook 6–8 minutes until browned.
3. Stir in diced eggplant and cook 5 minutes until soft.
4. Transfer beef mixture to a small baking dish. Top with mashed cauliflower.
5. Bake for 10 minutes until hot and golden on top.

■ *Sprinkle with a little paprika or chopped parsley before serving.*

> *Nutritional Information (Per Serving):* **Calories: 510 kcal | Protein: 24g | Fat: 17g | Carbs: 20g | Fiber: 8g | Net Carbs: 12g**

SPINACH & FETA STUFFED SWEET POTATOES WITH GARLIC YOGURT

🔔 1 serving   ● 25 min   ● Oven + Stovetop

INGREDIENTS:

1 small sweet potato (120g / ~4.2oz)
1 cup fresh spinach, chopped (30g / ~1oz)
1 oz feta cheese, crumbled (30g / ~1oz)
1/4 cup plain Greek yogurt (60g / ~2.1oz)
1 tbsp olive oil (15ml / ~0.5oz)

Also needed (not counted as main):
1 garlic clove, minced (3g / ~0.1oz)
Salt and pepper to taste
1/4 tsp cumin (0.5g / ~0.018oz)

INSTRUCTIONS:

1. Microwave or oven-bake sweet potato until soft (10–15 min). Slice open and fluff the flesh.
2. While baking, heat olive oil in a pan. Sauté spinach with garlic for 2–3 minutes until wilted.
3. In a small bowl, mix yogurt, cumin, salt, and pepper.
4. Stuff sweet potato with spinach and feta. Drizzle with garlic yogurt.

■ *Add toasted pine nuts on top for extra crunch and flavor.*

> *Nutritional Information (Per Serving):* **Calories: 495 kcal | Protein: 19g | Fat: 16g | Carbs: 28g | Fiber: 9g | Net Carbs: 19g**

CHAPTER 16: Comfort Dinners Everyone Will Love

CREAMY POLENTA WITH ROASTED MUSHROOMS & GARLIC OIL

🔔 1 serving 🟢 25 min 🟢 Oven + Stovetop

INGREDIENTS:

1/4 cup dry instant polenta (40g / ~1.4oz)
1 cup unsweetened almond milk (240ml / ~8.5oz)
1/2 cup mushrooms, sliced (75g / ~2.6oz)
1 tbsp extra virgin olive oil (15ml / ~0.5oz)
1 tbsp grated Parmesan cheese (7g / ~0.25oz)

Also needed (not counted as main):
1 garlic clove, minced (3g / ~0.1oz)
Salt and pepper to taste
1 tsp chopped fresh parsley (2g / ~0.07oz)

INSTRUCTIONS:

1. Roast mushrooms with oil, salt, and pepper at 400°F (200°C) for 12–15 min.
2. Simmer almond milk, whisk in polenta, cook 5 min. Add Parmesan, salt, and pepper.
3. Sauté garlic in oil until golden.
4. Serve polenta with mushrooms, garlic oil, and parsley.

▪ *Add a soft-boiled egg or wilted spinach for extra richness and nutrition.*

> *Nutritional Information (Per Serving):* **Calories: 485 kcal** | **Protein: 19g** | **Fat: 17g** | **Carbs: 28g** | **Fiber: 7g** | **Net Carbs: 21g**

LENTIL STEW WITH CARROTS, TOMATO & OREGANO

🔔 1 serving 🟢 30 min 🟢 Stovetop

INGREDIENTS:

1/2 cup cooked brown lentils (100g / ~3.5oz)
1/2 medium carrot, diced (40g / ~1.4oz)
1/3 cup canned diced tomatoes, no salt added (80g / ~2.8oz)
1 tbsp olive oil (15ml / ~0.5oz)
1 tbsp chopped onion (15g / ~0.5oz)

Also needed (not counted as main):
1 garlic clove, minced (3g / ~0.1oz)
1/2 tsp dried oregano (1g / ~0.035oz)
1/4 tsp ground cumin (0.5g / ~0.018oz)
Salt and pepper to taste
1 tbsp chopped fresh parsley (3g / ~0.1oz)

INSTRUCTIONS:

1. Heat olive oil in a pot over medium heat. Sauté onion, garlic, and carrot for 5 min until softened.
2. Stir in lentils, tomatoes, oregano, cumin, salt, and pepper. Simmer covered for 15–20 minutes, stirring occasionally.
3. Add a splash of water if stew becomes too thick. Serve hot, garnished with fresh parsley.

▪ *For extra creaminess, mash a few lentils into the broth before serving.*

> *Nutritional Information (Per Serving):* **Calories: 495 kcal** | **Protein: 21g** | **Fat: 15g** | **Carbs: 29g** | **Fiber: 9g** | **Net Carbs: 20g**

QUINOA & ROASTED CHICKEN BOWL WITH TAHINI DRESSING

🔔 1 serving   ● 25 min   ● Stovetop + Oven

INGREDIENTS:

1/2 cup cooked quinoa (90g / ~3.2oz)
4 oz cooked chicken breast, shredded (115g / ~4oz)
1/2 cup steamed broccoli florets (75g / ~2.6oz)
1 tbsp tahini (15g / ~0.5oz)
1 tbsp olive oil (15ml / ~0.5oz)

Also needed (not counted as main):
1 tsp lemon juice (5ml / ~0.17oz)
1 garlic clove, minced (3g / ~0.1oz)
Salt and pepper to taste
1 tbsp chopped parsley (3g / ~0.1oz)

INSTRUCTIONS:

1. Mix tahini, olive oil, lemon juice, garlic, salt, and pepper in a small bowl. Thin with a splash of water if needed.
2. In a serving bowl, arrange warm quinoa, chicken, and steamed broccoli.
3. Drizzle with tahini dressing and garnish with chopped parsley.

■ *Add a few toasted pumpkin seeds or a pinch of chili flakes for crunch and spice.*

Nutritional Information (Per Serving): **Calories: 535 kcal | Protein: 25g | Fat: 17g | Carbs: 28g | Fiber: 8g | Net Carbs: 20g**

PASTA WITH SARDINES, CAPERS & TOASTED BREADCRUMBS

🔔 1 serving   ● 25 min   ● Stovetop

INGREDIENTS:

2 oz whole wheat spaghetti (55g / ~1.9oz)
1 can sardines in olive oil, drained (3 oz / 85g)
1 tbsp capers, rinsed (10g / ~0.35oz)
1 tbsp olive oil (15ml / ~0.5oz)
2 tbsp whole grain breadcrumbs, toasted (15g / ~0.5oz)

Also needed (not counted as main):
1 garlic clove, minced (3g / ~0.1oz)
1/4 tsp chili flakes (0.5g / ~0.018oz)
Salt and black pepper to taste
1 tbsp chopped fresh parsley (3g / ~0.1oz)

INSTRUCTIONS:

1. Cook pasta according to package directions. Drain, reserving 2 tbsp pasta water.
2. In a skillet, heat olive oil. Add garlic and chili flakes, sauté 30 seconds.
3. Add sardines and capers, breaking sardines into pieces. Stir in cooked pasta and reserved water.
4. Toss to coat, top with toasted breadcrumbs and parsley.

■ *Use lemon zest or juice to balance the rich flavors of the sardines.*

Nutritional Information (Per Serving): **Calories: 510 kcal | Protein: 22g | Fat: 16g | Carbs: 30g | Fiber: 7g | Net Carbs: 23g**

BAKED COD WITH CHICKPEAS, TOMATO & SPINACH SAUCE

🔔 1 serving ● 25 min 💧 Oven + Stovetop

INGREDIENTS:

4 oz cod fillet, skinless (115g / ~4oz)
1/2 cup canned chickpeas, rinsed (80g / ~2.8oz)
1/3 cup canned crushed tomatoes (80g / ~2.8oz)
1 cup fresh spinach, chopped (30g / ~1oz)
1 tbsp olive oil (15ml / ~0.5oz)

Also needed (not counted as main):
1 garlic clove, minced (3g / ~0.1oz)
1/4 tsp smoked paprika (0.5g / ~0.018oz)
Salt and black pepper to taste
1 tsp lemon juice (5ml / ~0.17oz)

INSTRUCTIONS:

1. Preheat oven to 375°F (190°C). Season cod with salt, pepper, and paprika.
2. In a skillet, heat olive oil. Sauté garlic for 30 seconds, then add crushed tomatoes and chickpeas. Simmer for 5 minutes.
3. Stir in spinach until wilted. Transfer to a baking dish and place cod on top.
4. Bake for 12–15 minutes until cod flakes easily. Drizzle with lemon juice and serve.

▎ *Add a few capers or olives to the sauce for a briny depth.*

> *Nutritional Information (Per Serving):* **Calories: 495 kcal | Protein: 24g | Fat: 16g | Carbs: 26g | Fiber: 8g | Net Carbs: 18g**

FARRO RISOTTO WITH BUTTERNUT SQUASH & TOASTED PINE NUTS

🔔 1 serving ● 30 min 💧 Stovetop

INGREDIENTS:

1/3 cup semi-pearled farro, cooked (75g / ~2.6oz)
1/2 cup diced butternut squash (80g / ~2.8oz)
1 tbsp grated Parmesan cheese (7g / ~0.25oz)
1 tbsp toasted pine nuts (10g / ~0.35oz)
1 tbsp olive oil (15ml / ~0.5oz)

Also needed (not counted as main):
1 garlic clove, minced (3g / ~0.1oz)
1/4 tsp ground nutmeg (0.5g / ~0.018oz)
Salt and pepper to taste
1 tbsp chopped fresh parsley (3g / ~0.1oz)

INSTRUCTIONS:

1. Heat olive oil in a pot. Add garlic and diced squash. Sauté 5–6 minutes until tender.
2. Stir in cooked farro, nutmeg, salt, and pepper. Add a splash of warm water or broth to loosen, then stir in Parmesan.
3. Cook for 2–3 minutes until creamy. Top with toasted pine nuts and parsley.

▎ *Swap pine nuts for toasted walnuts or pumpkin seeds for variety.*

> *Nutritional Information (Per Serving):* **Calories: 540 kcal | Protein: 19g | Fat: 17g | Carbs: 29g | Fiber: 9g | Net Carbs: 20g**

BROCCOLI & CAULIFLOWER GRATIN WITH HERBED YOGURT DRIZZLE

🔔 1 serving ● 25 min ● Oven

INGREDIENTS:

1 cup broccoli florets (90g / ~3.2oz)
1 cup cauliflower florets (90g / ~3.2oz)
1/4 cup shredded part-skim mozzarella (30g / ~1oz)
1/4 cup plain Greek yogurt (60g / ~2.1oz)
1 tbsp olive oil (15ml / ~0.5oz)

Also needed (not counted as main):
1 garlic clove, minced (3g / ~0.1oz)
1 tbsp chopped fresh parsley or dill (3g / ~0.1oz)
Salt and pepper to taste
1 tbsp lemon juice (15ml / ~0.5oz)

INSTRUCTIONS:

1. Preheat oven to 400°F (200°C). Toss broccoli and cauliflower with olive oil, salt, and pepper.
2. Spread veggies in a small baking dish. Roast for 12–15 minutes until just tender.
3. Top with shredded cheese and return to oven for 5 minutes to melt.
4. In a bowl, mix yogurt, lemon juice, garlic, herbs, salt, and pepper.
5. Drizzle yogurt sauce over hot gratin and serve immediately.

■ Add 1 tbsp toasted walnuts or sunflower seeds for crunch and extra fiber.

> *Nutritional Information (Per Serving):* **Calories: 495 kcal | Protein: 21g | Fat: 17g | Carbs: 21g | Fiber: 8g | Net Carbs: 13g**

BULGUR PILAF WITH GROUND TURKEY & ROASTED VEGETABLES

🔔 1 serving ● 30 min ● Skillet + Oven

INGREDIENTS:

1/3 cup cooked bulgur (70g / ~2.5oz)
3 oz lean ground turkey (85g / ~3oz)
1/2 small zucchini, diced (60g / ~2.1oz)
1/4 red bell pepper, chopped (50g / ~1.8oz)
1 tbsp olive oil (15ml / ~0.5oz)

Also needed (not counted as main):
1 garlic clove, minced (3g / ~0.1oz)
1/2 tsp dried oregano (1g / ~0.035oz)
Salt and pepper to taste
1 tbsp chopped fresh mint or parsley (3g / ~0.1oz)

INSTRUCTIONS:

1. Preheat oven to 400°F (200°C). Toss zucchini and bell pepper with 1/2 tbsp olive oil and roast 12–15 minutes.
2. In a skillet, heat 1/2 tbsp olive oil. Sauté garlic and turkey with oregano, salt, and pepper until cooked through, 6–7 minutes.
3. Stir in bulgur and roasted vegetables. Cook together for 2–3 minutes to combine flavors.
4. Garnish with herbs and serve warm.

■ Add a spoonful of plain yogurt or lemon zest on top for brightness.

> *Nutritional Information (Per Serving):* **Calories: 525 kcal | Protein: 24g | Fat: 16g | Carbs: 27g | Fiber: 9g | Net Carbs: 18g**

GNOCCHI WITH TOMATO-BASIL SAUCE & CRUMBLED FETA

🔔 1 serving   🟢 20 min   🟢 Stovetop

INGREDIENTS:

2/3 cup cooked potato gnocchi (120g / ~4.2oz)
1/3 cup canned crushed tomatoes (80g / ~2.8oz)
1 oz feta cheese, crumbled (30g / ~1oz)
1 tbsp olive oil (15ml / ~0.5oz)
2 tbsp chopped fresh basil (4g / ~0.14oz)

Also needed (not counted as main):
1 garlic clove, minced (3g / ~0.1oz)
Salt and black pepper to taste
Pinch of chili flakes (optional)

INSTRUCTIONS:

1. Cook gnocchi in salted boiling water according to package instructions. Drain.
2. In a skillet, heat olive oil. Add garlic and sauté for 30 seconds.
3. Stir in crushed tomatoes, basil, salt, pepper, and chili flakes (if using). Simmer for 5 minutes.
4. Add gnocchi and toss to coat in the sauce.
5. Serve hot, topped with crumbled feta and extra basil.

■ Add a few halved cherry tomatoes for texture and sweetness.

Nutritional Information (Per Serving): **Calories: 510 kcal | Protein: 19g | Fat: 16g | Carbs: 28g | Fiber: 7g | Net Carbs: 21g**

WARM BARLEY & EGGPLANT BOWL WITH LEMON-PARSLEY OIL

🔔 1 serving   🟢 30 min   🟢 Stovetop + Oven

INGREDIENTS:

1/3 cup cooked pearl barley (75g / ~2.6oz)
1/2 cup roasted eggplant, cubed (80g / ~2.8oz)
1 tbsp olive oil (15ml / ~0.5oz)
1 tbsp grated Parmesan (7g / ~0.25oz)
1 tbsp chopped parsley (3g / ~0.1oz)

Also needed (not counted as main):
1 tsp lemon juice (5ml / ~0.17oz)
Salt and pepper to taste
1 garlic clove, finely minced (3g / ~0.1oz)

INSTRUCTIONS:

1. Roast cubed eggplant at 400°F (200°C) for 15–18 minutes until tender.
2. In a small pan, heat olive oil. Add garlic, lemon juice, parsley, salt, and pepper. Remove from heat.
3. Combine warm barley with roasted eggplant and Parmesan.
4. Drizzle with lemon-parsley oil and toss gently before serving.

■ Add a spoonful of Greek yogurt on top for creaminess and extra protein.

Nutritional Information (Per Serving): **Calories: 495 kcal | Protein: 20g | Fat: 15g | Carbs: 29g | Fiber: 8g | Net Carbs: 21g**

CHAPTER 17: Gather & Share — Weekend Table Meals

CHICKEN THIGHS WITH ARTICHOKES, LEMON & BABY POTATOES

🔔 1 serving   ● 30 min   ● Oven + Skillet

INGREDIENTS:

1 boneless skinless chicken thigh (4 oz / 115g)
1/2 cup baby potatoes, halved (90g / ~3.2oz)
1/3 cup canned artichoke hearts, quartered (60g / ~2.1oz)
1 tbsp olive oil (15ml / ~0.5oz)
1 tsp lemon juice (5ml / ~0.17oz)

Also needed (not counted as main):
1 garlic clove, minced (3g / ~0.1oz)
1/2 tsp dried oregano (1g / ~0.035oz)
Salt and black pepper to taste
1 tbsp chopped fresh parsley (3g / ~0.1oz)

INSTRUCTIONS:

1. Roast potatoes with oil, oregano, salt, and pepper at 400°F (200°C) for 15–20 min.
2. Sear chicken in a skillet, 4–5 min per side.
3. Add garlic and artichokes, sauté 2 min, then drizzle with lemon juice.
4. Serve with potatoes and parsley.

■ Add lemon zest or a few olives for bright, briny flavor.

> *Nutritional Information (Per Serving):* **Calories: 520 kcal | Protein: 24g | Fat: 17g | Carbs: 26g | Fiber: 8g | Net Carbs: 18g**

SPICED LAMB PATTIES WITH CUCUMBER SALAD & YOGURT SAUCE

🔔 1 serving   ● 25 min   ● Skillet

INGREDIENTS:

3 oz ground lamb (85g / ~3oz)
1/2 cup diced cucumber (70g / ~2.5oz)
1/4 cup plain Greek yogurt (60g / ~2.1oz)
1 tbsp olive oil (15ml / ~0.5oz)
1 tbsp chopped fresh mint (3g / ~0.1oz)

Also needed (not counted as main):
1/4 tsp ground cumin (0.5g / ~0.018oz)
1 garlic clove, minced (3g / ~0.1oz)
Salt and black pepper to taste
1 tsp lemon juice (5ml / ~0.17oz)

INSTRUCTIONS:

1. Mix lamb with cumin, garlic, salt, and pepper. Form 2 small patties.
2. Heat olive oil in a skillet and cook patties 4 minutes per side until browned and cooked through.
3. In a bowl, mix yogurt, lemon juice, and mint.
4. Toss cucumber with a pinch of salt. Plate with lamb patties and yogurt sauce.

■ Add thinly sliced red onion or a dash of paprika to the salad for extra flavor.

> *Nutritional Information (Per Serving):* **Calories: 495 kcal | Protein: 22g | Fat: 16g | Carbs: 14g | Fiber: 7g | Net Carbs: 7g**

ROASTED VEGETABLE PLATTER WITH CHICKPEA PURÉE & PITA

🔔 1 serving   ● 30 min   ● Oven + Blender

INGREDIENTS:

1/2 cup canned chickpeas, rinsed (80g / ~2.8oz)
1/2 small zucchini, sliced (60g / ~2.1oz)
1/2 red bell pepper, sliced (50g / ~1.8oz)
1/4 small eggplant, cubed (60g / ~2.1oz)
1/2 small whole wheat pita (30g / ~1.1oz)
1 tbsp olive oil (15ml / ~0.5oz)

Also needed (not counted as main):
1 garlic clove, minced (3g / ~0.1oz)
1 tbsp lemon juice (15ml / ~0.5oz)
1/2 tsp ground cumin (1g / ~0.035oz)
Salt and pepper to taste

INSTRUCTIONS:

1. Preheat oven to 400°F (200°C). Toss zucchini, pepper, and eggplant with 1/2 tbsp olive oil, salt, and pepper. Roast 15–18 min.
2. In a blender, blend chickpeas, lemon juice, garlic, cumin, 1/2 tbsp olive oil, and 2 tbsp water until smooth.
3. Warm pita and serve with purée and roasted vegetables.

■ *Sprinkle with smoked paprika or fresh parsley before serving.*

> *Nutritional Information (Per Serving):* **Calories: 525 kcal | Protein: 19g | Fat: 16g | Carbs: 30g | Fiber: 9g | Net Carbs: 21g**

ZUCCHINI BOATS STUFFED WITH TURKEY, RICE & HERBS

🔔 1 serving   ● 30 min   ● Oven + Skillet

INGREDIENTS:

1 medium zucchini, halved and scooped (130g / ~4.6oz)
3 oz lean ground turkey (85g / ~3oz)
1/4 cup cooked brown rice (50g / ~1.8oz)
1 tbsp grated Parmesan (7g / ~0.25oz)
1 tbsp olive oil (15ml / ~0.5oz)

Also needed (not counted as main):
1 garlic clove, minced (3g / ~0.1oz)
1 tbsp chopped fresh parsley or mint (3g / ~0.1oz)
Salt and black pepper to taste

INSTRUCTIONS:

1. Preheat oven to 375°F (190°C).
2. Sauté garlic and turkey in 1/2 tbsp oil for 5–6 min until cooked. Stir in rice, herbs, salt, and pepper.
3. Stuff zucchini halves with the mixture. Top with Parmesan and drizzle with 1/2 tbsp oil.
4. Bake for 15–18 min until tender and golden.

■ *Add a spoonful of plain Greek yogurt on top for creaminess.*

> *Nutritional Information (Per Serving):* **Calories: 495 kcal | Protein: 22g | Fat: 15g | Carbs: 27g | Fiber: 8g | Net Carbs: 19g**

SEAFOOD STEW WITH TOMATO, GARLIC & FRESH PARSLEY

🛎 1 serving   ● 25 min   🌿 Stovetop

INGREDIENTS:

3 oz cod fillet, cut into chunks (85g / ~3oz)
3 oz peeled shrimp (85g / ~3oz)
1/2 cup canned crushed tomatoes (120g / ~4.2oz)
1/4 cup chopped celery (30g / ~1oz)
1 tbsp olive oil (15ml / ~0.5oz)

Also needed (not counted as main):
1 garlic clove, minced (3g / ~0.1oz)
1 tbsp chopped fresh parsley (3g / ~0.1oz)
Salt and black pepper to taste
1/4 tsp smoked paprika (0.5g / ~0.018oz)
1/2 cup water or low-sodium vegetable broth (120ml / ~4.2oz)

INSTRUCTIONS:

1. Heat olive oil in a pot. Sauté garlic, celery, and paprika for 2–3 min.
2. Add crushed tomatoes, water or broth, salt, and pepper. Simmer 5 min.
3. Add cod and shrimp. Cover and simmer 6–8 min until seafood is cooked through.
4. Stir in fresh parsley and serve hot.

▮ *Serve with lemon wedge or a drizzle of extra virgin olive oil for brightness.*

> *Nutritional Information (Per Serving):* **Calories: 495 kcal | Protein: 25g | Fat: 15g | Carbs: 18g | Fiber: 8g | Net Carbs: 10g**

BAKED EGGPLANT ROLLS WITH RICOTTA & BASIL MARINARA

🛎 1 serving   ● 30 min   🌿 Oven

INGREDIENTS:

1/2 medium eggplant, sliced lengthwise (100g / ~3.5oz)
1/4 cup ricotta cheese (60g / ~2.1oz)
1/3 cup canned tomato sauce (80g / ~2.8oz)
1 tbsp grated Parmesan (7g / ~0.25oz)
1 tbsp olive oil (15ml / ~0.5oz)

Also needed (not counted as main):
1 garlic clove, minced (3g / ~0.1oz)
1 tbsp chopped fresh basil (3g / ~0.1oz)
Salt and pepper to taste

INSTRUCTIONS:

1. Preheat oven to 400°F (200°C). Brush eggplant slices with 1/2 tbsp oil. Roast for 10–12 min until tender.
2. In a bowl, mix ricotta, Parmesan, garlic, salt, and pepper.
3. Spread tomato sauce in a baking dish. Fill each eggplant slice with ricotta mixture, roll up, and place seam-side down.
4. Spoon extra sauce on top, drizzle with remaining oil. Bake 10–12 min. Garnish with fresh basil.

▮ *Add chili flakes or chopped spinach to the ricotta for more flavor.*

> *Nutritional Information (Per Serving):* **Calories: 520 kcal | Protein: 21g | Fat: 16g | Carbs: 22g | Fiber: 8g | Net Carbs: 14g**

GRILLED TUNA WITH FARRO, SPINACH & OLIVE TAPENADE

🔔 1 serving ● 25 min 🌿 Grill + Stovetop

INGREDIENTS:

4 oz tuna steak (115g / ~4oz)
1/3 cup cooked farro (75g / ~2.6oz)
1 cup fresh spinach (30g / ~1oz)
1 tbsp olive tapenade (20g / ~0.7oz)
1 tbsp olive oil (15ml / ~0.5oz)

Also needed (not counted as main):
1 tsp lemon juice (5ml / ~0.17oz)
Salt and black pepper to taste
1 garlic clove, minced (3g / ~0.1oz)

INSTRUCTIONS:

1. Season tuna with salt and pepper. Grill 2–3 min per side for medium-rare.
2. In a skillet, sauté garlic in 1/2 tbsp olive oil. Add spinach and cook until wilted.
3. Toss farro with remaining oil and lemon juice.
4. Plate farro, top with spinach, grilled tuna, and olive tapenade.

■ *Add lemon zest or fresh herbs for extra flavor.*

> *Nutritional Information (Per Serving):* **Calories: 540 kcal | Protein: 25g | Fat: 17g | Carbs: 26g | Fiber: 8g | Net Carbs: 18g**

FAMILY TRAY BAKE WITH SAUSAGE, ONIONS & WHITE BEANS

🔔 1 serving ● 30 min 🌿 Oven

INGREDIENTS:

1 chicken or turkey sausage, sliced (85g / ~3oz)
1/2 cup canned white beans, rinsed (90g / ~3.2oz)
1/2 small red onion, sliced (40g / ~1.4oz)
1/4 red bell pepper, sliced (50g / ~1.8oz)
1 tbsp olive oil (15ml / ~0.5oz)

Also needed (not counted as main):
1 garlic clove, minced (3g / ~0.1oz)
1/2 tsp dried rosemary or thyme (1g / ~0.035oz)
Salt and pepper to taste

INSTRUCTIONS:

1. Preheat oven to 400°F (200°C).
2. Toss sausage, beans, onion, and bell pepper with olive oil, garlic, herbs, salt, and pepper.
3. Spread on a tray and roast 20–25 min, stirring once halfway.
4. Serve warm with fresh herbs if desired.

■ *Add a drizzle of balsamic glaze before serving for depth.*

> *Nutritional Information (Per Serving):* **Calories: 510 kcal | Protein: 22g | Fat: 16g | Carbs: 28g | Fiber: 9g | Net Carbs: 19g**

GREEK-STYLE BAKED RICE WITH CHICKEN AND ROASTED PEPPERS

🛎️ 1 serving ⏱️ 25 min 🔥 Oven

INGREDIENTS:

4 oz boneless skinless chicken breast, diced (115g / ~4oz)
1/2 cup cooked brown rice (90g / ~3.2oz)
1/4 cup roasted red bell pepper, sliced (40g / ~1.4oz)
1/4 cup diced zucchini (40g / ~1.4oz)
1 tbsp crumbled feta cheese (15g / ~0.5oz)
1 tbsp olive oil (15ml / ~0.5oz)

Also needed (not counted as main):
1 small garlic clove, minced (3g / ~0.1oz)
1/4 tsp dried oregano (0.5g / ~0.02oz)
Salt and pepper to taste

INSTRUCTIONS:

1. Preheat oven to 375°F (190°C).
2. Sauté chicken and garlic in olive oil for 5–6 min until lightly golden.
3. Add zucchini and peppers; cook 2–3 min.
4. Stir in rice, oregano, and a pinch of salt and pepper.
5. Transfer mixture to a small baking dish, sprinkle with feta.
6. Bake for 8–10 min until heated through and cheese softens.

▪ *Add a squeeze of lemon juice or fresh dill just before serving to brighten the flavor.*

> *Nutritional Information (Per Serving):* **Calories: 495 kcal | Protein: 24g | Fat: 17g | Carbs: 29g | Fiber: 8g | Net Carbs: 21g**

CAULIFLOWER & CHICKPEA TAGINE WITH CINNAMON & APRICOT

🛎️ 1 serving ⏱️ 30 min 🔥 Stovetop

INGREDIENTS:

3/4 cup cauliflower florets (90g / ~3.2oz)
1/3 cup canned chickpeas, rinsed (80g / ~2.8oz)
2 dried apricots, chopped (15g / ~0.5oz)
1 tbsp tomato paste (15g / ~0.5oz)
1 tbsp olive oil (15ml / ~0.5oz)

Also needed (not counted as main):
1/4 tsp ground cinnamon (0.5g / ~0.02oz)
1 small garlic clove, minced (3g / ~0.1oz)
Salt and black pepper to taste
Water or broth as needed

INSTRUCTIONS:

1. Heat olive oil in a skillet over medium. Sauté garlic and cinnamon 1 min.
2. Add cauliflower and chickpeas. Stir in tomato paste and 2 tbsp water or broth.
3. Simmer covered for 15–18 min until tender.
4. Add apricots in the final 5 min.
5. Season with salt and pepper and serve warm.

▪ *Garnish with chopped parsley and a spoonful of Greek yogurt for balance and richness.*

> *Nutritional Information (Per Serving):* **Calories: 520 kcal | Protein: 19g | Fat: 16g | Carbs: 30g | Fiber: 9g | Net Carbs: 21g**

CHAPTER 18: Grocery Planning for Mediterranean Success

Lasting change doesn't happen by accident — it happens by design. That's why this book offers not only flavorful Mediterranean recipes and a complete 30-day meal plan but also smart, structured grocery shopping lists to make healthy living simple, enjoyable, and stress-free.

Each weekly shopping list is thoughtfully crafted to match the recipes in your daily meal plan, giving you clear direction on what to buy, how much to prep, and how to keep your kitchen stocked with everything you need for success — without overspending, overbuying, or wasting food.

Here's what makes these lists different:

Organized by category for faster, easier shopping trips

Focused on fresh, wholesome Mediterranean ingredients — not ultra-processed foods

Practical quantities tailored for individuals, couples, or families

Smart ingredient cross-usage to minimize waste and maximize variety

Aligned with the core values of the Mediterranean lifestyle: balance, simplicity, and real food

These aren't just shopping lists — they're tools for consistency and success. By planning ahead, you'll save time, stay energized, and make every meal a celebration of health and flavor.

And because flexibility is part of the Mediterranean spirit, you can personalize each list to reflect your tastes, local markets, or seasonal produce — all while staying true to the nourishing, heart-healthy principles of this time-honored way of eating.

Let these lists guide your grocery cart, simplify your routine, and help you bring the vibrant flavors of the Mediterranean to your table — effortlessly and deliciously.

Grocery Shopping List for 7-Day Meal Plan

Meat & Poultry:
Chicken breast – 1.5 lb / 680 g (Grilled Chicken with Artichokes, Chicken & Orzo Skillet)
Ground turkey – 1 lb / 450 g (Turkey Ragù, Turkey Meatballs)
Lamb – 1 lb / 450 g (Skillet Lamb with Spinach, Lamb Chops)
Chicken thighs – 1 lb / 450 g (One-Dish Chicken and Orzo)

Fish & Seafood:
Salmon fillets – 1.5 lb / 680 g (Grilled Salmon with Quinoa, Roasted Salmon with Lentils)
Shrimp – 12 oz / 340 g (Shrimp & Chickpea Bake, Mediterranean Shrimp Skewers)
Cod fillets – 10 oz / 300 g (Baked Cod with Herbed Couscous)
Tuna – 1 small can (Orzo Salad with Tuna)

Vegetables:
Spinach (fresh) – 4 bunches (Shakshuka, Chickpea Hash, Salmon with Spinach)
Tomatoes – 10 medium (Tomato Confit, Lentil Salad, Meatball Tray)
Red bell peppers – 3 medium (Bulgur Bowl, Chickpea Bake)
Eggplant – 2 large (Eggplant Bake, Eggplant Stack)
Zucchini – 3 large (Zucchini Pancakes, Shrimp Bake)
Mushrooms – 8 oz / 225 g (Mushroom Tartlets, Polenta with Mushrooms)
Asparagus – 1 bunch (Cottage Cheese Bowl)
Garlic – 1 bulb (Various recipes)
Red onion – 2 large (One-Pan Chicken, Skillet Lamb)

Lemons – 5 medium (Salmon, Chicken, Shrimp, Dressings)
Potatoes – 4 medium (Lemon Garlic Chicken)
Kalamata olives – 1 small jar (Mediterranean Salads)
Cucumber – 2 medium (Couscous Salad)

Fruits:
Apples – 4 medium (Baked Pears, Farro with Apples)
Oranges – 3 medium (Citrus Salads, Orange Yogurt)
Berries (fresh or frozen) – 2 cups / 300 g (Parfait, Millet with Berries)
Figs (fresh or dried) – 1 cup / 150 g (Baked Figs, Fig Compote)
Plums – 3 medium (Yogurt Parfait)
Dried apricots – 6 oz / 175 g (Couscous Dessert)
Grapes – 1 small bunch (Roasted Grapes with Labneh)
Lemons – 2 extra (Snacks, Dressings)
Mint – 1 small bunch (Various dishes)

Grains & Bread:
Quinoa – 1.5 cups / 270 g (Quinoa Salad, Quinoa Bowl)
Couscous – 1 cup / 180 g (Couscous Bowls, Couscous Dessert)
Farro – 1 cup / 180 g (Farro Salad, Farro Breakfast)
Millet – 1 cup / 180 g (Millet Breakfast, Millet Pudding)
Bulgur – 1 cup / 180 g (Bulgur Pilaf, Bulgur Patties)
Orzo – 1 cup / 180 g (Orzo Salad, Chicken Orzo Skillet)
Whole grain bread or pita – 4 slices or pitas (Olive Toast, Vegetable Wraps)

Dairy & Eggs:
Feta cheese – 10 oz / 280 g (Zucchini Pancakes, Salads, Stuffed Peppers)
Parmesan cheese – 6 oz / 170 g (Zucchini Pasta, Casseroles)
Greek yogurt (plain, full-fat) – 2 cups / 500 g (Parfaits, Dips)
Labneh or cream cheese – 8 oz / 225 g (Smoked Salmon, Desserts)
Ricotta cheese – 8 oz / 225 g (Baked Pears, Ricotta Cream)
Eggs – 18 large (Breakfasts, Shakshuka, Polenta)

Nuts, Seeds & Nut Butter:
Almonds (whole or chopped) – 1 cup / 150 g (Desserts, Parfaits)
Walnuts – ½ cup / 75 g (Fig Clusters, Salad Toppings)
Pine nuts – ¼ cup / 50 g (Zucchini Pancakes)
Chia seeds – ½ cup / 75 g (Millet Porridge, Chia Pudding)
Pistachios – ½ cup / 75 g (Freekeh, Mousse)

Pantry Staples:
Olive oil (extra virgin) – 1 bottle (Various recipes)
Honey – 1 small jar (Desserts, Dressings)
Tahini – 1 jar (Lentil Bowl, Couscous Bowl)
Dijon mustard – 1 small jar (Salad Dressing)
Herbs & spices (oregano, za'atar, sumac, cinnamon) – variety for seasoning

Grocery Shopping List for 8-14 Day Meal Plan

Meat & Poultry:
Chicken breast – 1.5 lb / 680 g (One-Pan Chicken with Zucchini, Grilled Chicken Salad)
Ground turkey – 1 lb / 450 g (Turkey & Vegetable Ragù, Turkey Stuffed Zucchini Boats)
Lamb – 1 lb / 450 g (Skillet Lamb with Chickpeas, Spiced Lamb Patties)
Chicken thighs – 1 lb / 450 g (One-Pan Chicken, Chicken with Artichokes)

Fish & Seafood:
Salmon fillets – 1.5 lb / 680 g (Grilled Salmon with Yogurt Sauce, Salmon Tray Bake)
Shrimp – 12 oz / 340 g (Sheet-Pan Shrimp, Shrimp & Chickpea Bake)
Cod fillets – 10 oz / 300 g (Baked Cod with Couscous)
Tuna (canned) – 1 small can (Orzo Salad with Tuna)

Vegetables:
Spinach (fresh) – 4 bunches (Shakshuka, Lamb Skillet, Salmon with Spinach)
Tomatoes – 10 medium (Eggplant Bake, Tomato Confit, Tabouli, Salads)
Red bell peppers – 3 medium (Vegetable Platters, Couscous Salad)
Eggplant – 2 large (Baked Eggplant Rolls, Eggplant Stacks)
Zucchini – 3 large (Zucchini Boats, Ratatouille, Sheet-Pan Shrimp)
Mushrooms – 8 oz / 225 g (Polenta with Mushrooms, Vegetable Bake)
Asparagus – 1 bunch (Vegetable Sides)
Garlic – 1 bulb (Various recipes)
Red onion – 2 large (Chicken Orzo, Vegetable Bake)
Lemons – 6 medium (Shrimp, Salmon, Chicken, Salads, Dressings)

Potatoes – 4 medium (Tray Bake, Chicken with Potatoes)
Kalamata olives – 1 small jar (Salads, Couscous)
Cucumber – 2 medium (Cucumber Salad, Quinoa Bowls)

Fruits:
Apples – 4 medium (Farro with Apples, Desserts)
Oranges – 3 medium (Citrus Salads, Orange Yogurt, Rosewater Desserts)
Berries (fresh or frozen) – 2 cups / 300 g (Parfaits, Millet with Berries)
Figs (fresh or dried) – 1 cup / 150 g (Fig Clusters, Desserts)
Plums – 3 medium (Yogurt Parfaits)
Dried apricots – 6 oz / 175 g (Couscous Dessert, Tagine)
Grapes – 1 small bunch (Roasted Grapes with Labneh)
Watermelon – 1 small (Watermelon Salad)
Mint – 1 small bunch (Various dishes)
Basil – 1 small bunch (Eggplant Rolls, Salads)

Grains & Bread:
Quinoa – 1.5 cups / 270 g (Quinoa Salad, Chicken Quinoa Bowl)
Couscous – 1 cup / 180 g (Couscous Salads, Stuffed Peppers)
Farro – 1 cup / 180 g (Farro with Apples, Farro Risotto)
Millet – 1 cup / 180 g (Millet Pudding, Breakfast Bowls)
Bulgur – 1 cup / 180 g (Bulgur Salad, Pilaf)
Orzo – 1 cup / 180 g (Chicken & Orzo Skillet, Orzo Salad)
Whole grain pita or bread – 4 slices or pitas (Olive Toast, Vegetable Platter)

Dairy & Eggs:
Feta cheese – 10 oz / 280 g (Stuffed Peppers, Salads, Stuffed Potatoes)
Parmesan cheese – 6 oz / 170 g (Zucchini Pasta, Casseroles)
Greek yogurt (plain, full-fat) – 2 cups / 500 g (Parfaits, Sauces)
Labneh or cream cheese – 8 oz / 225 g (Salmon, Dessert Toppings)
Ricotta cheese – 8 oz / 225 g (Eggplant Rolls, Pear Desserts)
Eggs – 18 large (Breakfasts, Shakshuka, Polenta)
Goat cheese – 6 oz / 170 g (Ratatouille, Appetizers)
Halloumi – 6 oz / 170 g (Grilled Halloumi Salad)

Nuts, Seeds & Nut Butter:
Almonds (whole or chopped) – 1 cup / 150 g (Desserts, Parfaits)
Walnuts – ½ cup / 75 g (Salads, Fig Desserts)
Pistachios – ½ cup / 75 g (Freekeh, Mousse)
Chia seeds – ½ cup / 75 g (Puddings, Parfaits)
Pine nuts – ¼ cup / 50 g (Vegetable Platters)

Pantry Staples:
Olive oil (extra virgin) – 1 bottle (Various recipes)
Honey – 1 small jar (Desserts, Salads)
Tahini – 1 jar (Dips, Grain Bowls)
Dijon mustard – 1 small jar (Dressings, Chicken)
Herbs & spices (oregano, za'atar, sumac, cumin, cinnamon, basil) – variety for seasoning

Grocery Shopping List for 15-21 Day Meal Plan

Meat & Poultry:
Chicken breast – 1.5 lb / 680 g (Chicken & Orzo Skillet, Mediterranean Meatball Tray)
Ground turkey – 1 lb / 450 g (Turkey & Vegetable Ragù, Turkey Meatballs)
Lamb – 1 lb / 450 g (Skillet Lamb & Couscous, Spiced Lamb Patties)
Chicken thighs – 1 lb / 450 g (One-Pan Chicken with Vegetables, Chicken with Potatoes)

Fish & Seafood:
Salmon fillets – 1.5 lb / 680 g (Salmon Tray Bake, Grilled Salmon with Yogurt Sauce)
Shrimp – 12 oz / 340 g (Shrimp & Chickpea Bake, Sheet-Pan Shrimp)
Cod fillets – 10 oz / 300 g (Baked Cod with Tomato Sauce)
Tuna (canned) – 1 small can (Orzo Salad with Tuna)

Vegetables:
Spinach (fresh) – 4 bunches (Shakshuka, Lamb Skillet, Salmon with Spinach)
Tomatoes – 10 medium (Tomato Confit, Salads, Cod with Tomatoes)
Red bell peppers – 3 medium (Vegetable Platters, Couscous Salad)
Eggplant – 2 large (Eggplant Bake, Shepherd's Pie, Stuffed Zucchini Boats)
Zucchini – 3 large (Zucchini Boats, Ratatouille, Skillet Dishes)

Mushrooms – 8 oz / 225 g (Polenta with Mushrooms, Pasta)
Asparagus – 1 bunch (Vegetable Sides)
Garlic – 1 bulb (Various recipes)
Red onion – 2 large (Chicken Orzo, Vegetable Platters)
Lemons – 6 medium (Shrimp, Chicken, Salmon, Salad Dressings)
Potatoes – 4 medium (Tray Bake, Chicken with Potatoes, Shepherd's Pie)
Kalamata olives – 1 small jar (Couscous Salad, Fish)
Cucumber – 2 medium (Cucumber Salad, Grain Bowls)

Fruits:
Apples – 4 medium (Farro with Apples, Desserts)
Oranges – 3 medium (Citrus Salads, Orange Yogurt, Rosewater Sweets)
Berries (fresh or frozen) – 2 cups / 300 g (Parfaits, Millet Bowls)
Figs (fresh or dried) – 1 cup / 150 g (Baked Figs, Fig Clusters)
Plums – 3 medium (Yogurt Parfaits)
Dried apricots – 6 oz / 175 g (Couscous Dessert, Tagine)
Grapes – 1 small bunch (Roasted Grapes with Labneh)
Watermelon – 1 small (Watermelon Salad)
Mint – 1 small bunch (Various salads, dressings)
Basil – 1 small bunch (Eggplant Rolls, Pasta)

Grains & Bread:
Quinoa – 1.5 cups / 270 g (Quinoa Bowls, Chicken & Quinoa)
Couscous – 1 cup / 180 g (Couscous Bowls, Stuffed Peppers)
Farro – 1 cup / 180 g (Farro Risotto, Farro with Apples)
Millet – 1 cup / 180 g (Millet Breakfasts, Millet Pudding)
Bulgur – 1 cup / 180 g (Pilafs, Salads)
Orzo – 1 cup / 180 g (Chicken Orzo Skillet, Orzo Salads)
Whole grain pita or bread – 4 slices or pitas (Olive Toast, Vegetable Platters)

Dairy & Eggs:
Feta cheese – 10 oz / 280 g (Stuffed Peppers, Salads, Stuffed Sweet Potatoes)
Parmesan cheese – 6 oz / 170 g (Zucchini Pasta, Baked Casseroles)
Greek yogurt (plain, full-fat) – 2 cups / 500 g (Parfaits, Dips, Yogurt Sauces)
Labneh or cream cheese – 8 oz / 225 g (Smoked Salmon, Desserts)
Ricotta cheese – 8 oz / 225 g (Desserts, Eggplant Rolls)
Eggs – 18 large (Breakfasts, Shakshuka, Polenta)
Goat cheese – 6 oz / 170 g (Vegetable Platters, Ratatouille)
Halloumi – 6 oz / 170 g (Grilled Halloumi Salad)

Nuts, Seeds & Nut Butter:
Almonds (whole or chopped) – 1 cup / 150 g (Desserts, Parfaits, Tagine)
Walnuts – ½ cup / 75 g (Salads, Fig Desserts)
Pistachios – ½ cup / 75 g (Breakfast Bowls, Mousse)
Chia seeds – ½ cup / 75 g (Parfaits, Millet Bowls)
Pine nuts – ¼ cup / 50 g (Vegetable Platters)

Pantry Staples:
Olive oil (extra virgin) – 1 bottle (All dressings and cooking)
Honey – 1 small jar (Desserts, Salad Dressings)
Tahini – 1 jar (Grain Bowls, Couscous Salads)
Dijon mustard – 1 small jar (Chicken, Salads)
Herbs & spices (oregano, za'atar, sumac, cumin, cinnamon, basil) – variety for seasoning

Grocery Shopping List for 22-30 Day Meal Plan

Meat & Poultry:
Chicken breast – 1.5 lb / 680 g (Chicken with Artichokes, Quinoa Chicken Bowl)
Ground turkey – 1 lb / 450 g (Turkey Ragù, Stuffed Zucchini Boats)
Lamb – 1 lb / 450 g (Skillet Lamb with Couscous, Spiced Lamb Patties)
Chicken thighs – 1.5 lb / 680 g (Chicken with Baby Potatoes, Mediterranean Tray Bake)
Beef (lean ground) – 1 lb / 450 g (Shepherd's Pie, Beef & Eggplant Casserole)

Fish & Seafood:
Salmon fillets – 1.5 lb / 680 g (Grilled Salmon with Yogurt Sauce, Salmon Tray Bake)
Shrimp – 12 oz / 340 g (Shrimp & Chickpea Bake, Sheet-Pan Shrimp)
Cod fillets – 10 oz / 300 g (Baked Cod with Tomato Sauce)
Tuna (canned) – 1 small can (Orzo Salad with Tuna)

White fish (halibut or similar) – 12 oz / 340 g (Baked Halibut with Vegetables)

Vegetables:
Spinach (fresh) – 4 bunches (Shakshuka, Lamb Skillet, Stuffed Sweet Potatoes)
Tomatoes – 12 medium (Eggplant Bake, Tomato Sauce, Ratatouille, Salads)
Red bell peppers – 4 medium (Vegetable Platters, Couscous Salad, Stuffed Peppers)
Eggplant – 3 large (Eggplant Rolls, Shepherd's Pie, Stuffed Boats)
Zucchini – 4 large (Zucchini Boats, Ratatouille, Tray Bakes)
Mushrooms – 8 oz / 225 g (Polenta with Mushrooms, Vegetable Bake)
Asparagus – 1 bunch (Vegetable Sides)
Garlic – 1 bulb (Various recipes)
Red onion – 3 large (Vegetable Platters, Skillet Meals)
Lemons – 6 medium (Shrimp, Salmon, Chicken, Dressings, Desserts)
Potatoes – 5 medium (Tray Bake, Chicken with Potatoes, Shepherd's Pie)
Kalamata olives – 1 small jar (Salads, Fish Dishes, Grain Bowls)
Cucumber – 2 medium (Cucumber Salad, Grain Bowls)
Carrots – 3 medium (Stews, Roasts, Salads)
Fennel – 1 bulb (Baked Cod, Roasted Vegetables)

Fruits:
Apples – 4 medium (Desserts, Farro with Apples)
Oranges – 3 medium (Citrus Salad, Orange Yogurt, Rosewater Sweets)
Berries (fresh or frozen) – 2 cups / 300 g (Parfaits, Millet Bowls)
Figs (fresh or dried) – 1 cup / 150 g (Fig Compote, Desserts)
Plums – 3 medium (Yogurt Parfaits)
Dried apricots – 6 oz / 175 g (Couscous Dessert, Tagine)
Grapes – 1 small bunch (Roasted Grapes with Labneh)
Watermelon – 1 small (Watermelon Salad)
Mint – 1 small bunch (Salads, Dips, Dressings)
Basil – 1 small bunch (Eggplant Rolls, Pasta, Garnish)
Peach – 2 medium (Grilled Peach Dessert)

Grains & Bread:
Quinoa – 1.5 cups / 270 g (Quinoa Bowls, Chicken Quinoa)
Couscous – 1 cup / 180 g (Couscous Salads, Stuffed Peppers)
Farro – 1 cup / 180 g (Farro Risotto, Farro Bowls)
Millet – 1 cup / 180 g (Millet Pudding, Breakfast Bowls)
Bulgur – 1 cup / 180 g (Pilafs, Salads)
Orzo – 1 cup / 180 g (Chicken Orzo Skillet, Orzo Salads)
Whole grain pita or bread – 4 slices or pitas (Olive Toast, Platters, Side Dishes)
Brown rice – 1 cup / 180 g (Stuffed Peppers, Tagine)

Dairy & Eggs:
Feta cheese – 10 oz / 280 g (Stuffed Peppers, Salads, Sweet Potatoes)
Parmesan cheese – 6 oz / 170 g (Baked Pasta, Zucchini Gratin)
Greek yogurt (plain, full-fat) – 2 cups / 500 g (Parfaits, Sauces, Desserts)
Labneh or cream cheese – 8 oz / 225 g (Salmon, Desserts)
Ricotta cheese – 8 oz / 225 g (Eggplant Rolls, Pear Desserts)
Eggs – 18 large (Breakfasts, Shakshuka, Polenta)
Goat cheese – 6 oz / 170 g (Ratatouille, Stuffed Dishes)
Halloumi – 6 oz / 170 g (Grilled Halloumi Salad)
Mozzarella – 6 oz / 170 g (Baked Pasta, Mediterranean Platters)

Nuts, Seeds & Nut Butter:
Almonds (whole or chopped) – 1 cup / 150 g (Desserts, Parfaits, Tagine)
Walnuts – ½ cup / 75 g (Salads, Fig Desserts)
Pistachios – ½ cup / 75 g (Breakfast Bowls, Desserts)
Chia seeds – ½ cup / 75 g (Parfaits, Millet Bowls)
Pine nuts – ¼ cup / 50 g (Vegetable Platters, Salads)

Pantry Staples:
Olive oil (extra virgin) – 1 bottle (All cooking, dressings, dips)
Honey – 1 small jar (Desserts, Salads)
Tahini – 1 jar (Couscous Salads, Sauces)
Dijon mustard – 1 small jar (Dressings, Chicken)
Capers – 1 small jar (Fish Dishes, Dressings)
Herbs & spices (oregano, za'atar, sumac, cumin, cinnamon, thyme, basil, paprika) – variety for seasoning

Printed in Dunstable, United Kingdom